QUICKBOOKS

Guide To Master Bookkeeping And Accounting For Small Businesses And Simple Concept Technique Books

Scott McMoney

TABLE OF CONTENTS

INTRODUCTION

It is an act of accounting to count the money in your wallet or bag. You also perform a bookkeeping role if you ever notice how much you have. You still count things in daily life without worrying about accounting twice. For example, before setting the table at home, you count the plates. When you are out of town, you count the number of e-mails you receive. Even a move like looking at your watch and thinking about how long you have before your next appointment is an accounting process.

Accounting and accounting services include auditing, tax services, management consulting services, general accounting, cost accounting, budgeting, and internal auditing. Because your company is a non-profit organization, these programs are important to your everyday business. Your charity can't survive the long distance without them. Following that transparency, it is important to understand how to monitor and account for the daily activities of your non-profit. Keeping non-profit books is fun. Having federal grants to support the services alleviates financial stress. For your financial audit to have a clean health check adds credibility. I dedicate this book to all non-profits, which offer the sector credibility by keeping its books in order.

This book is a guide that you can gather from time to time for the following steps during your accounting cycle:

1. Your non-profit is entering into a second party agreement.
2. You or your workers create a business document, like a sales invoice, which leaves a paper trail.
3. In your first file, your journal, you or your employee records the transaction.
4. You add the transaction to the main directory.
5. You match the overall panel and plan a test score. Your reference balance checks the exactness of the account balances (debit and credit).
6. You are managing your accounts.

This book acts as a tool to help you achieve the ultimate goal of a well-organized and reliable financial statement, no matter where you are in the accounting process.

CHAPTER 1 : BOOKKEEPING BASICS

Many small business owners do not always like to carry out 'power' duties while loving to work in their chosen field. Many business owners tend to use the credentials of a professional bookkeeper. Some may want to give their accountant their bag full of receipts and hope that a useful set of accounts will come out at the end of the accounting carton! We help demystify the role of a bookkeeper in this book. You may just begin a business and therefore can't afford the services of a bookkeeper yet! Find this book as a checklist of jobs to be done.

The Basics

You probably have great ideas to run your own company like most business-people and just want to start up. However, you do not want to be distracted by the little things you're using, like keeping a detailed record of every penny you spend. Oh, you're not in a sprint; slow down! You can't measure the progress (or failure, unfortunately) of your business activities if you don't carefully plan your bookkeeping program and figure out exactly what financial details you want to track. When done correctly, bookkeeping gives you an outstanding indicator of how well you perform and offers plenty of knowledge all year round. Such information helps you test your business strategy's financial success and make any necessary adjustments to your income targets early in the year.

Basic Accounting Methods

You can't keep accounts when you learn how to do so by looking at basic accounting methods. The two primary forms of accounting are cash and accrual accounting. The main difference between these two approaches is how much sales and transactions you report in your accounts. You only report transactions when cash changes hands if you choose cash-based accounts. If you are using accrual accounting, even if the cash does not change hands, you report the transaction when it is done. SuForample, suppose that your company buys products for sale from a manufacturer but does not actually pay for these items for 30 days. If you use cash-based accounting, you will not report the payment until the supplier has actually deposited the cash. If the accounting is used, the payment is reported when you acquire the goods, and the future debt is documented in the Trade Creditors account. HM Revenue & Customs, which are interested in all UK companies, only support the accrual form of accounting. Therefore, you can't actually use a cash-based account. However, A special concession for smaller enterprises allows them to use a form of cash-based VAT accounting. In essence, on a cash-based accounting, you will complete your VAT return.

Understanding Capital, Liabilities, and Assets

A growing company has three key financial pieces that need to be kept in balance: assets, capital, and liabilities. Of course, those might be foreign concepts for some of you, so perhaps an accounting first is in order. We use the example of buying a house with a mortgage. The house you buy is an asset; that is, you own something of value. You don't all own it in the first year of the mortgage but by the end of the mortgage period (typically 25 years). The hypothecary is a liability or a debt you owe. As the years go by, and you decrease mortgage (liability), your capital or property ownership increases. In a nutshell, that's it. Assets include everything that the company owns, including cash, assets, houses, equipment, and vehicles. Capital includes claims on assets based on their site are of ownership of the company. Liabilities include all the companies owed to others, including supplier payments, the balance of credit cards, and bank loans.

The formula to balance the books includes these three elements:

Assets = Capital + Liabilities

Introducing Credits and Debits

You have to reform your thinking on two common financial terms: debits and loans in order to keep the books. Most non-bookkeepers and non-accountants find loans to be subtracted from their bank accounts. The opposite is true of credits-credits are generally regarded as modifications to their accounts, usually in the form of refunds or corrections for account holders. Okay, forget about everything you think you know about debits; double-entry bits and credits in the field of bookkeeping are entirely different species. Since bookkeeping requires double-entry bookkeeping, for every transaction, you must make at least two entries – a debit and a loan – in your bookkeeping system. It only depends on the type of transaction, whether the debit or credit adds or subtracts from an account. All this debit, credit, and double entrance sounds confusing, but we guarantee that this method will be much clearer as you work through the novel.

Diagraming Your Bookkeeping Course

Payments in books cannot just be performed willy-nilly. You will know exactly where these transactions fit in with the broader accounting system. To find out where it goes, use your Account Chart that essentially shows all the accounts your company has and the types of transactions you make.

Discovering Various Types of Business

Before you start up, you are wise to sit down and think about your business structure. For instance, if you are a window cleaner, if you see yourself just doing your own rounds and not working with anyone else, it would be more than acceptable if you start-up ole trader.

Controlling and Planning your Activities

Many businesses only start-up and trade from day to day without any real plan or control of the activities they conduct. Many businesspeople get so distracted that they constantly fight a fire and lack real direction. We like checklists because they help to coordinate the bookkeeping tasks in an organized and methodical way. This organizational degree helps you to store and update your accounts day by day or even week by week. You can always continue quickly and easily from where you left off.

Establishing Internal Controls

ways business owners must ensure that tight controls are kept on cash and the use of that cash. And one of the best ways of establishing this control is by placing internal restrictions on who can enter your books' information and who can use it. You also need to carefully control who can accept cash receipts and spend the cash of your business. The correct division of duties lets you protect your company's properties from errors, theft, and fraud.

Maintaining and Defining a Ledger

You may be confused with words such as magazines, books, articles, journals, and accounts. Most of these terms originated from conventional bookkeeping practices of handwritten records in big ledgers in cloth. These looked like papers, so bookkeeping is the term – keep financial records in the books! The books are also called journals or booklets (we told you that it was a bit confusing!). Typically, you would have one book for your sales, one for shopping, and a general one for all (often known as General Ledger). Often companies will keep a separate cash register, which tracks earned cash and paid cash. Many people now use computers to make their accounts (to help our busy lives). The easiest collection of records can be made on a table, but we do not encourage it since errors can be made easily, and you must have to find an appropriate way to balance accounts.

The word ledger is common to most computerized accounting systems:

Sales Ledger: A ledger with all individual customer accounts and balance sheets. Sometimes this directory is referred to as Customer Ledger or Debtors Ledger.

Purchase Ledger: A folder with all the accounts and balances of each manufacturer. This directory is sometimes known as the Ledger or Ledger suppliers.

Nominal document: A booklet that contains balances and events for all of the company's nominal accounts. This booklet is also known as the Ledger General.

Cashbook: In Sage, in particular, you can have a variety of current bank accounts and small cash accounts under the general heading 'Money.' In this section of the accounting system, any cash earned or paid is reported.

Accounts: Clearly, for all ledgers, a collective term. The nominal booklet is the core of your bookkeeping method. You keep in this book a list of all your accounts and the financial activities carried out during the year.,

You can use each Nominal Ledger account's balance to produce your monthly, quarterly, or annual financial reports. These account summaries can also be used to build internal relationships that help you make key business decisions.

Managing Daily Finances By Using Bookkeeping Tools

Daily Finance Management Bookkeeping Software After you set up your business books and enforce your internal controls, you are ready to use the systems you have built to handle your business 'day-to-day work. A well-structured bookkeeping system makes it much easier to handle the finances of your company.

Sales Monitoring

Everyone wants to know how good sales are. You can easily get the numbers on a daily basis if you keep your books up to date and reliable. You can also see sales patterns every day, weekly, or monthly if you deem appropriate. Use the information collected through the bookkeeping system to control sales, analyze customer promotions, and track product returns. All three elements are essential to ensure the quality of your products 'sales.

If you find that you have to offer discounts more often to increase sales, you might have to check the price, and you certainly have to research the market to determine the cause of this sales weakness. The trigger can be the violent competitor's latest practices or simply a slowdown in your specific market. In any case, you have to understand the problem and learn how to achieve your income goals given obstacles. If monitoring your sales reveals an increase in the number of items returned, you have to find the reason for this change. Perhaps the price of the commodity you are selling declines, and a new supplier must be sought.

Regardless of the reason, an increasing number of product returns typically indicates a problem to be addressed and remedied.

Keeping Stock

If your company holds stock in hand or warehouses, it is important to track the costs of the goods to be sold to maintain your profit potential. You may have to change your own prices to preserve your profit margin when you see stock costs escalating. You definitely won't wait to see how much your stock costs you until the end of the year. You must also watch carefully how much stock you have and how much has been sold. Stock can get lost, discarded, or stolen, so your actual inventory counts that differ from the counts you have in your accounts. Conduct physical counts on a regular basis – for most businesses at least monthly and perhaps for some retail stores regularly. In addition to looking for signs of robbery or bad product management, make sure you have ample stock available to meet customers 'needs.

When you run a service-based company, you should count yourself lucky because your business doesn't have a huge stock expense. You mainly sell time and use material stocks as part of your business. However, you can not disregard the inventory costs so that you obtain the same lessons on stock management.

Running Accuracy Checks

Monitoring or tracking transactions is time-consuming if you do not routinely check to ensure you have correctly entered certain transactions. The old adage 'Garbage in, garbage out' is especially true for bookkeeping: if the numbers you place in your bookkeeping system are waste, the reports that you produce are also waste.

Checking the Cash and Bank

The first step in the checking of your accounts includes evidence of the integrity of your cash transactions. It includes checking numerous transactions and products, including your employees 'regular cash and the integrity of your bank account(s).

Checking your Balance

After you prove that your cash is correct, you can check that everything else has been reported just as precisely in your accounts. Check the accounts for any flagrant mistakes and then evaluate if a trial balance is in order or not.

Making Bookkeeping Corrections

You will need to make additional changes after you have reached your usual daily purchases, such as accruals, prepayments, and depreciation.

Financial Reports Preparation

Most businesses plan at least two key financial reports: a profit and loss statement and a balance sheet. These reports can be shown to others, including financial institutes from which the company borrows money and investors.

The Balance sheet shows the financial health of your company as of a given date. Ideally, it shows that your company's assets are equivalent to the value of your liabilities and capital.

The balance sheet is referred to as the balanced formula-

Assets = Capital + Liabilities

The profit and loss statement summarizes the financial transactions of your company for a specific period, such as a month, quarter, or year. This financial statement begins with your revenues, subtracts the costs of the goods sold, and subtracts all costs for running the business. The profit and loss statement shows how much the company profited during the accounting period. If you haven't done well, the statement Profit and Loss shows how much you have lost.

Computers now play an important role in your report production. If your nominal codes have been properly set up, you can easily prepare reports by clicking on the button! Having said all this, you need to understand the double-entry bookkeeping rules. So when you have to change your books, you have the requisite confidence to complete newspapers by following the two-way bookkeeping rules.

Payroll Handling

Payroll management can be an incredible problem for many corporations. You have to comply with dozens of legislative and fiscal legislation and complete a great deal of paperwork. They must also take care to collect and pay for things such as pay as you work (pay as you earn) and national insurance. And you have another layer of recordkeeping to deal with when you pay employee benefits.

Works with your Accountant

Most accountants are ideal for providing a statement on profit and loss and balance sheet, but they may not prefer accounting methods used by a business, for example, stock valuation and the measurement of the cost of goods sold.

That said, the organization relies in the first place on a competent bookkeeper to manage its financial records. The bookkeeper may be the first company owner. And, if you buckle up, we're on a bookkeeping trip!

KNOWING MORE ABOUT BOOKKEEPING

All companies have to keep track of their financial transactions, and that is why bookkeeping and bookkeeping are so important.

How can you say, without accurate records, if your business is profiting or losing?

Bookkeeping: Record-Keeping of Business World

Bookkeeping is the technique used by companies to track their financial transactions. Accounting is the entire system of documents and procedures for the documentation, analysis, and reporting of the financial transactions of an entity. Bookkeeping includes the documentation of financial information in the accounting system while following sound accounting principles.

The bookkeeper's job is to work every day to ensure that transactions are properly reported. Bookkeepers must be accurate and enjoy working with numbers as they deal with numbers and accounts throughout the day because they deal with numbers and accounts throughout the day.

Bookkeepers don't have to be members of a recognized professional body, such as the England and Wales Chartered Accountants Institute. You may identify a chartered accountant by lettering ACA by email, showing that she is a member of the Chartered Accountants Institute. If she's trained any longer, she may use the FCA letters that indicate that the accountant is a Chartered Accountants Institute Fellow. For example, both Scotland and Ireland are licensed with their own chartered accounting bodies. There are other accounting credentials available from Chartered Accountants Institute (ACMA and

FCMA), Chartered Certified Accountants Institute (ACCA and FCMA), and Chartered Accountants Institute (CIPFA). There are several other accounting qualifications. The Association of Accounting Technicians offers an ABC program that provides an excellent basis for this subject. In fact, most bookkeepers seem to be experienced. If you are looking for help from an accountant, then use the right chartered accountant or a chartered certified accountant because they have the most relevant experience. Many small business owners act as their own bookkeepers as soon as the organization is large enough to hire a dedicated person to keep the accounts. Few small companies have payroll accounts for reviewing records and preparing official financial reports. They instead have bookkeepers (who are paid or self-employed) who represent the eyes and ears of external accountants. Most companies look for an accountant, normally a chartered accountant (ACA or FCA), but typically do so to record annual reports in domestic profits, which now forms part of HM Revenue & Customs. In many small firms today, a bookkeeper enters the business every day while working in the company. The bookkeeper gives a summary report at the end of each month or quarter to the bookkeeper, who then tracks the consistency of his transactions and prepares financial statements, including profit and loss and balance sheet reports. The accounting system is initially developed with the aid of an accountant in most situations. The goal is to ensure that the system uses sound accounting principles and that their analyzes are compatible with what is expected by the client, the accountant, and HM Revenue

& Customs. The accountant regularly checks the use of the program to ensure that the workers manage transactions properly.

Precise financial reports are the only way you know how your business is doing. Your company produces these reports by using the details you put into your accounting system as a bookkeeper. If this is not valid, your financial report does not have any meaning: note, 'waste inside, waste out.'

Until you can take on bookkeeping and start keeping accounts, you first need to get a grip on the main accounting requirements. Each segment explains the basic terms used every day by all bookkeepers.

Bookkeeping Terminologies

Listed below are a few terms and terminologies you need to know:

Balance Sheet: A variety of words you need to know: balance sheet: a financial statement showing a snapshot of the financial position of the company (assets, liabilities, and capital) at a specific time. The balance sheet is so-called because the company's items (assets) have to be equal to claims against such properties.

The total assets on an ideal balance sheet must be equal to the total liabilities plus the total capital. If your numbers suit the format, the books of the organization are balanced.

Assets: All products of a business, such as cash, inventory, debtors, buildings, property, machinery, equipment, vehicles, and mobilization.

Liabilities: All of the company's obligations, such as mortgages, loans, and unpaid bills.

Capital: All the money that business owners spend on the enterprise. When an individual (solo trader) or a group of persons (partnerships) own a small business, the capital of the owner is shown on the capital account. The wealth of the shareholder is shown as shares in a company (limited corporation).

Another essential capital account is Retrained Profits, which indicates all the business profit is reinvested in the enterprise instead of being dividends to the shareholders. Unincorporated companies show money paid off to the owners in a drawing account (or separate drawing accounts for a partnership). At the same time, firms distribute money to their investors by paying dividends (a percentage of the company profits, usually for the year, paid to the ordinary shareholders).).

Profit and Loss Statements

The following are some terms and conditions relating to the profit and loss statement you need to be aware of:

Profit and Loss Statement: Financial statement offering a description over a certain period of time, such as a month, quarter, or year of the company's financial operation. The statement begins with sales made, deducting the product's selling and purchase costs– net profit or loss.

Income: All profits made during the selling of the products and services of the company. Some businesses often generate revenue through other ways, such as the sale of goods not required by the company or the income from investments.

Expenses of goods Sold: All costs incurred for the purchase or manufacture of products or services to be offered to its customers.

Expenses: All the costs incurred by the business not directly related to the selling of particular goods or services.

Other Common Terms

Some other common words include:

Accounting Periods: Time for the preparation of financial information. Many businesses track their financial results on a monthly basis so that each accounting cycle is equivalent to one month. Some businesses choose to generate quarterly financial reports, so the accounting duration is three months. Many firms review their reports quarterly only, with an accounting duration of 12 months. Enterprises that track their financial activities monthly often produce quarterly and annual reports (a review of the activities and financial results of the business year-end) based on information collected.

Accounting year-end: The accounting year in most cases is twelve months and is twelve months after the beginning of the year or at a typical point in the business cycle. Most companies hold year-ends of 31 March (to match the tax year) and 31 December (to tie the calendar year). You can change your business year-end to suit your company. For example, if you began on July 1, your year-end is June 30 (12 months later). But if historically your industry is 31 December as the year-end, you are quite to move to that date. For example, 31 December is the year-end for most retailers. Of course, you must notify HM Revenue & Customs and seek its formal approval.

Commercial Debtors (also known as Receivable Accounts): The system used to chart all consumer transactions on credit. Payment does not apply to credit card transactions, rather purchases where the company gives a customer credit directly, and which the company must receive at a later date from the buyer.

Trade Creditors (also known as Payable Accounts): The account used to track any bills outstanding from manufacturers, vendors, consultants, and other companies or individuals from whom the company buys goods or services.

Depreciation: An accounting tool for the aging and use of assets. For example, if you buy a car, you know that the value of the car decreases every year (except if you buy one of those classic cars that are more worthwhile). Any important asset of a company, including buildings, plants, equipment, and other main items, has age and eventually needs replacement.

Nominal Ledger: A directory that lists all the accounts of the company. The Nominal Ledger is the central bookkeeping program summary.

Inventory: The account that controls all goods sold to customers.

Journals: Where bookkeepers maintain track of everyday business transactions (in chronological order). Each of the most active accounts has its own journal, including Currency, Trade Creditors, and Trade Debtors.

Payroll: The way a company pays its workers. Managing the payroll is the bookkeepers 'core task, which includes reporting to HM Revenue & Customs various facets of their payroll, including taxes incurred on behalf of the employee and employer, as well as NICs (National Insurance Contributions). Furthermore, there may be a host of other fees, such as Statutory Sick Pay (SSP) and maternity/paternity pay.

Trial Balance: How to check the books in balance before gathering financial report information and closing books for the accounting period.

Scaling Through the Accounting Cycle

You conclude the business by performing the accounting cycle activities as a bookkeeper so called because the process is circular: transactions entered, the transactions processed through the accounting cycle, and the books closed -at-the end of the accounting period.

1. ***Transactions:*** The cycle starts with the financial transactions. Selling or returning a commodity can be included in transactions, buying arrangements for business purposes, or any other financial operation requiring the exchange of assets of the company; setting up or paying off debt; or depositing or making payments of money to owners of the enterprise. Both revenue and expenditures must be reported as transactions. They address more comprehensive transactions in the book by explaining how basic business practices can be documented – revenue reporting, acquisitions, asset acquisition or disposal, new debt collection, or debt payments.

You add the transactions to the account concerned. All accounts are contained in the Nominal Ledger, where all the accounts of the company can be listed. A computerized accounting system records the correct debits and credits to the right accounts automatically. For instance, if an invoice for the purchase is entered as a transaction for British

Telecom, the Ledger is credited, and the Nominal telephone account is debited.

1. ***Reconciliations:*** You must update your bank account(s) and ensure that your bank entries have been correctly reported until you have completed all your transactions.
2. ***Trial balance:*** You are planning a trial balance at the end of the accounting period (which could be a month, quarter, or year depending on the business practice). You must then check every Trial Balance account to ensure that it is correct.
3. ***Adjusting the journal entries:*** You would have to make changes to certain accounts after checking the trial balance in order to make corrections. You also have to pay for asset depreciation and compensate for one-time payments (such as insurance). These must be distributed annually in order to balance monthly expenses with monthly revenues more effectively. After you make the changes, run another Trial Balance to make sure you're satisfied with the accounts.
4. ***Financial statements:*** You are using the revised balance sheet and profit and loss statement.
5. ***Book closure:*** You close the Revenue and Expense accounts books and start the whole process again. All financial reports are closed at the end of the fiscal year (year-end). This means that income and expense accounts will begin at the beginning of the new accounting year

with a zero balance. In comparison, the company carries over the balance of assets, liabilities, and resources from year to year, so the business doesn't begin every period by selling old assets and purchasing new assets, repaying and then taking on debts or settling all claims for the owners and retrieving the money again.

Understanding Various Accounting Strategies

Most non-profit entities, such as sports teams, have very basic accounting requirements. While being responsible for the safe care of their subscriptions and other assets, such organizations are not accountable to shareholders for their financial results. Consequently, the accounting emphasis is not on income calculation but rather on receipts and payments accounting. In this situation, a simple cash-based accounting system might well be enough to allow only cash transactions – it is not necessary to give or receive credit.

However, complications may occur in the current accounting year when members do not pay their dues, and this circumstance must be reflected in their accounts. In this case, the correct approach is accrual accounting (see the later "Recording of accrual accounting immediately").

Some businesses operate on a cash basis, and their owners may provide a strong case for using this process. However, many accountants and HM Customs & Revenue do not support this approach as there is no precise calculation of income (or loss) over time. In this coming chapter, we will briefly explain how cash-based accounting operates before it is discarded in favor of the more appropriate form of accrual.

Understanding the Limitations of Cash-based Accounting

For cash-based accounting, you report all transactions on paper when cash changes hands, i.e., when the company receives a cash payment from the clients or pays cash for sales or other services. Cash receipt or payment may be by means of cash, cheque, credit card, e-transfer, or other payment methods used for the item.

Cash accounting cannot be used when a company sells credit items and collects money later from the consumer. There is no provision in the cash-based accounting method documenting and monitor customer money at any future time.

This also refers to transactions. The cash accounting method only documents the purchasing of products or items to be sold later if it actually pays cash. When the company buys credit items to be charged later, the transaction is only reported if the cash is actually paid out.

You may want to start with cash-based accounts, depending on the size of your company. Most small businesses run by a single owner or a small group of investors use the simpler cash-based accounting method. If your business model is easy – you don't have stock, start, finish, and pay for each job in a single accounting period- cash-based accounting will work for you. As the business grows, however, you may need to turn to accrual accounting to better track revenue and expenses and meet the requirements of the external accountants and HM Revenue & Customs. The same fundamental argument applies to non-profit organizations.

Cash-based accounting works well in monitoring cash flow, but the program does a poor job of matching cash revenues. This deficiency is a problem, especially when a business buys goods in a month and sells them in the next month.

Say you buy goods in June and pay $1,000 in cash to sell the same month. You will not sell the items until July, when you collect cash for the transactions. When you close your books at the end of June, you have to report $1,000 without any profits, so you lose that month. If you sell the goods in July for $1,500, you have a profit of $1,500. Your monthly June report shows a loss of $1,000, and your monthly July report shows a profit of $1,500, when in fact you had profits of $500 over the two months. With cash-based accounting, you can never be certain that you have an exact income or loss figure, but because non-profit organizations use cash-based accounting, it is not shocking.

Since accrual accounts are the only appropriate accounting system for accountants and HM Revenue & Customs, we focus on this approach in the whole book. Do not worry when you choose to use cash-based accounting because you own a cash-only company and a straightforward trading model: most of the bookkeeping information is still useful, but you do not have to hold other accounts, such as trade debtors and business creditors, since you don't report transactions before cash changes hands. You'd better track what people owe you if you're using a cash-based accounting system and start selling things in credit.

Our recommendation is to use the accrual approach from the outset. You need more detailed and legally needed accrual accounting when your business is that and your business model changes.

Using Accrual Accounting

Through accrual accounting, all transactions should be reported as they occur, and though no cash changes hands. For example, if you sell a credit, you immediately record and enter the transaction into a Trade Debtors account before you obtain payment. You enter the transaction in a Trade Creditors account immediately when you purchase products on credit before you pay out cash.

Unlike cash, accrual accounting has a disadvantage: it does a good job of balancing income and expenditure, but it does a poor job of monitoring cash. Because you report the income when the transaction takes place and not when you raise the cash, the profit and loss statement will look fantastic even though you have no cash in the bank. For example, suppose you run a contracting company and complete jobs every day. When the job is done, you will report income, even though you have not yet earned the cash. However, you can end up with a lot of income but little cash when your customers are slow to pay. Recall – never equate benefit with cash. Cash-flow is somewhat more important than profit in the short term, but profit is more important in the long term.

Most businesses that use the cumulative accounting method track cash flow every week to ensure that they have adequate cash in hand to run the company. When your business is seasonal, for example, a landscape company with nothing to do during the winter months, you can set up short-term loans through your bank in order to maintain your cash flow through the lean times.

Double-Entry Bookkeeping

Every business use Double-Entry Controlling to hold their accounts, whether they are using the cash form or the accrual form of accounting. Double-entry accounting – so named because you enter all transactions twice – eliminates mistakes and increases the likelihood of balancing the accounts.

The central formula for the balance sheet (assets = liabilities + capital) plays an important role in double-entry book management.

Essential Rules of Bookkeeping

You have some basic rules to follow when dealing with double-entry bookkeeping. Second, note that a debit is on the left-hand side of a ledger, and credit is on the right side. Then the following rules apply:

- If you want an asset to be increased, debit the Account Value.
- You must credit the Assets account to decrease an asset.
- You are crediting the Liabilities account to increase your responsibility.
- You are debiting the Liabilities account to decrease responsibility.
- You debit the Expense account if you want to report an expense.
- You pay the expense account if you need an expense reduction.
- You credit the payroll account if you want to report profits.
- You debit the payroll account if you want to reduce your payroll.

Here's a realistic example in practice. Suppose you buy a new office desk which costs $1.500. In fact, this transaction consists of 2 parts: you spend an asset (cash) on another asset (mobilizing). Therefore, you have to change two accounts to the company books: the cash and the mobilizer account. A bookkeeping transaction is as follows:

Account ***Debit*** ***Credit***

Furniture $1,500

Cash $1,500

In this transaction, you will be able to report the accounts affected by a loan to buy a new office desk. The debit-increases the value of the Furniture account, and the value of the cash account decreases. Both accounts impacted by this transaction are asset accounts. Seeing how the balance sheet is affected, you can see that the only changes are made on the asset side of the equation:

Assets = Liabilities + Capital

Furniture increase = No change on this side of the equation cash decrease.

In this situation, the books stay in balance because the same amount of sterling pounds increase the value of your Furniture account decreases the balance sheet's value. Have a brief description at the end of that journal entry that describes the intent of the article. In the first example, we suggested that this entry was 'To buy a new office desk.'

Practicing With This Example:

I will show you how you report a transaction that affects the Balance Sheet equation on both sides. Here is an example that records stock purchasing. Suppose you buy 5,000 dollars of credit widgets. (What widgets do you always talk about? Don't help. They just serve as examples of what is bought when something is of no real importance.) All these new widgets add value to your Stock Asset account, as well as add value to your Trade Creditors account. The bookkeeping process for your widget purchase looks like this:

Account	***Debit***	***Credit***
Stock	$5,000	
Trade Creditors		$5,000

For buying widgets for sale to customers

This transaction affects the balance sheet equation as follows:

Assets = Liability + Capital

Stock increases = No change + Creditor increases

From the two examples, you can see how double-entry bookkeeping helps to balance the books as long as you ensure each entry in the books is balanced. Balancing the entries may seem straightforward, but bookkeeping entries sometimes become complicated when the transaction involves more than two accounts.

Cash Accounting and Accrual Accounting

The approaches for tracking and documenting the revenues and expenditures you heard about in the last chapter are two distinct. The selection of your company's system is an important decision that must be made very early in the life of your company. Once it has been created, the legalities of IRS make it difficult to alter.

All forms are (1) cash and (2) accrual accounts. In the following pages, I clarify how and when revenues and expenditures are reported using each method and show you some of the advantages and inconveniences associated with each method.

"CASH" AND "ACCRUAL" ACCOUNTING

Cash Accounting

The documentation of your profits and expenses when they are actually received or compensated. A business using the cash accounting system shall be deemed to have made a purchase whether the cash is obtained directly or paid out for services or goods.

Accrual Accounting

The identification of sales and expenditures as obtained or incurred irrespective of whether the cash is collected or paid out for the transaction.

Two examples showing the difference

1. ***Revenue transaction/Sales***

ABC Company paid XYZ Client $500 for consulting services on January 16th. On 5 February, XYZ Business paid the invoice.

Method of accounting used:

- ***Cash basis:*** No record-keeping entry is needed on 16th January because there was no cash exchange between the two companies. Until payment is issued in February, ABC Company shall not report sales. It is then registered and considered a sale in February.
- ***Accrual basis:*** ABC Company documents its selling on 16 January, given the fact that no cash has been exchanged. ABC Corporation is deemed to have received revenue on the 16th of January (the date of invoice) even though it does not collect cash until the 5th of February. In other words, it's a deal in January.

1. ***Purchase-transaction.***

ABC Business received $125.32 in the Office Super Store on January 25. At the end of the month, Office Super Store bills ABC Business. On 10 February, ABC Company charges the invoice.

Method of accounting used:

- ***Cash basis:*** No recordkeeping entry is made by ABC Business on 25 January because it did not exchange cash with Office Super Store. ABC Company does not report the costs until payment is made on 10 February. The transaction shall be taken into account in February.

- ***Accrual basis:*** ABC Company reports the expenses on 25 January, but it has not exchanged cash with the Office Super Store. ABC Company is considered to have paid the expense of the office supplies on the 25th of January, but ABC will not pay them until the 10th of February. The transaction is expressed in January costs.

Which Method Would You Prefer to Use?

The most common strategy used by businesses is cash because it is the easiest and most straightforward way to deal with. Nevertheless, the IRS mandates that all company forms take advantage of the accrual accounting basis.

"The IRS notes that, if the business revenue is generated by the selling of the product (retailers, wholesalers, suppliers, etc.), you will use the form accrual to account for purchases and sales." Simply put, if your business profits are generated by selling the products, you will have to record profit and expenditures using the accrual form on your tax return.

Many conditions generally apply to accrual accounting. C Corporations and companies with gross receipts of more than $5 million usually use the accrual approach as their total tax accounting method, even according to IRS requirements.

There are some specific situations under which an organization may have to use this form or be excluded from it.

Consult with Your Tax Accountant

I'll give you some of the advantages and disadvantages of both approaches. Nonetheless, in order to determine most intelligently whether your business wants to use the accrual basis or the cash basis for your reporting and record-keeping process, it would be prudent to consult with your tax advisor, who will explain the criteria and help you make your decision.

Advantages and Disadvantages of the Two Methods

Advantages:

Cash Basis

- Simpler all forms
- Allows one-stop accounting to be used
- Taxes charged only in cash actually earned.

Accrual Basis

- Provides a great analytical method, as revenues and expenditures correspond closely to the actual transaction duration.

Disadvantages:

Cash Basis

- Does not correlate closely to revenues and expenses with the actual transaction duration.

Accrual Basis

- It needs a more complicated accounting replication scheme.
- The income tax is paid on taxes invoiced.

Can You Change Methods Yearly?

You must pick a system and stick with it for IRS purposes. Personally, I would encourage you to consult your tax professional before setting up your records and choose the approach to do your best to satisfy the IRS as you file the tax returns for you.

Expenses and Income

Small business accounting is based on one assumption. Each transaction involves money received, invested, infused, or removed from the company. All revenue and money spent on business are listed under one of two: profits (or income) and expenses. Before you build your records, some basic facts about both words must be remembered.

- ***Income (Or Revenue)***

Earnings are the money that your company earns in any given period. This consists of retail revenue, wholesale purchases, service revenues, interest income, and numerous other incomes.

You'll want to make sure you don't mix sales and expenditures. You will not use the money earned to buy goods and intend to deposit the balance under any situation. A simple tax accounting rule requires your profits to be equal to your deposits. However, it is so imperative to note that if you follow this approach, the IRS does not demand that you retain copies of your receipt book. The tax reform of 1986 promotes the profit alternative to the deposit equation.

- ***Expenses***

Costs are all the money that your company pays out. They include check payments and cash payments. All require careful documentation. Expenditure is classified into four different categories, namely.

Cost of goods sold (inventory)

- Cost of goods or inventories sold over a period of accounting.
- Includes work and equipment, or the purchase price of the goods manufactured.

Variables expenses

- Such costs are directly linked to the selling of your product or service.
- Includes marketing costs, production salaries, distribution, development and research, manufacturing, sales and wages, vehicle expenditures, equipment, and any other overhead products or services.

Fixed (administrative) expenses

- These are costs not directly linked to your production or service delivery. They are the kind of costs that all companies share.
- Such expenses include daily office overhead such as accounting and legal fees, bank fees, banking fees, payroll expenses, leases, permits, banking facilities, office equipment, telecommunications, utility services, insurance, etc. Administrative costs usually remain unchanged if the company stops production or services unexpectedly for a while.

Other expenses

- Interest charges.
- Requires money spent on transactions, loans, etc.

Note: Other types of expenditures can be divided into administrative and selling expenditures. Types are:

- ***Utilities/Providers.*** Those used for manufacturing as distinguished from office services, heating, toilets, etc.
- ***Phone.*** Telemarketing and advertisement are costs for sale. Monthly payments and office telephone charges are operating expenses.
- ***Freight and postal services.*** Shipping your product is a selling expense. The postage that is used as an overhead office is an administrative cost.

The groups in which those costs are to be placed may be confusing. It is important to remember that somewhere all expenses have to be registered. If a sales expense is wrongly reported as an administrative expense, it will have no serious impact. However, you will have a good basis to evaluate the company and implement changes if you can identify the cost information correctly.

What are Deductible Expenses?

Deductible expenses are the expenditures allowed by the IRS when you, at the end of your company tax year, compute the net profit(s) or taxable income. To pay the least amount of income tax to increase your own gains, you have to familiarize yourself with the deductible costs by statute.

Popular Deductible Expenses

A list of products that are typically deductible for income tax purposes can be found on the following link. The new company owner will be acquainted with the right ones. DO NOT wait until you see this list for tax preparation time. Knowing in advance what expenditures are deductible would help you to use them while preserving the right records for verification of income tax and business analysis. Know this is just a partial list. There may well be additional deductible costs for your product. Call or IRS meet. You have free publications to answer a lot of your questions. Your accountant is another source of information.

Make sure that all expenditures are reported in order to check if you are audited.

Is deductible absolutely or depreciable?

Expenses fall into two major categories:

- All deductibles in full in the year in which they occur
- Depreciated and deferred products for a specified number of years.

1. ***Completely deductible expenditures:*** All expenses incurred in your company shall be deductible for the year in which they arise, and your net profit shall be diminished by the sum thereof unless they are significant costs falling into the category of depreciable assets. Expenses would have to be listed for tax purposes, and receipts for verification will be readily recoverable.
2. ***Depreciable expenses:*** When you buy a business property with an expected life period of more than one year that is not planned for resale, the property is considered depreciable. The expense (generally over $100) shall be calculated for more than a year, and a depreciation deduction shall be asserted over the useful life or recovery period of the property. Such types of material assets include structures, cars, machinery, and equipment and intangible property such as copyrights or franchises. Depreciation shall take place at a fixed rate.

This part is deducted as an expense for the current year. Under Section 179 of the Code, you may opt not to view all or part of the cost of such qualified properties as a depreciable income but as an expense. The average expense for a tax year you can choose to subtract has been raised in 2005 to $102,000 and in 2006 to $108,000. This cap shall extend to each taxpayer and not to each taxpayer's company.

Caution: Make sure that you do not list all deductible and depreciable assets at the same expense as any purchase. For example, if you have bought and depreciated a computer for $3,000, make sure it is not also reported as the maximum deductible cost for office equipment. However, it is so prudent to maintain a separate list of all depreciable expenditures and allow the fiscal accountant to determine whether each item should be expensed or depreciated under Section 179.

Popular Deductible Expenses

Publishing: Yellow pages, magazines, radio, clear fax, etc.

Bad debts: Sales or services

Bank charges: Checks

Books and periodicals: Business-related

Car and truck-related expenses: Petrol, maintenance services. Licensing, insurance

Commissions: Sales rep

Contract Services – independent

Convention Expenses

Display and Exhibit Expenses

Donations

Dues – professional

Educational Fees and Materials

Electric Bills

Entertainment of Clients

Freight – UPS, FedEx, Postal, etc.

Gas Bills

Improvements – under $100

Insurance – business-related

Interest Paid Out

Laundry/Cleaning – uniforms, etc.

Legal and Professional Fees

License Fees – business license

Maintenance – material and labor

Office Equipment – under $100

Office Furniture – under $100

Office Supplies

Parking Fees

Pension and Profit-Sharing Plans

Postage

Printing Expenses

Professional Services

Promotional Materials

Property Tax

Publications

Rent

Repairs

Refunds,

And Allowances

Sales Tax

Telephone

Tools

Uniforms Purchased

Utilities

Wages Paid Out

Summarily, at this point, you can very well find the implementation of accrual accounting and cash accounting methods confusing. But because the correct approach is the early decision you would have to make on the timing of your revenue and expenditures tracking and reporting, I feel that it was a good idea to get to know the definition.

Once you have chosen the accrual or cash basis for your record-keeping, you will be able to go to the next segment, where you can find out about the total documents the business keeps.

WHY BOOKKEEPING IS IMPORTANT FOR SMALL BUSINESSES

Reasons Why book-keeping is important for maintaining accurate financial records. However, many small businesses still fail to implement this integral process. In addition to maintaining correct books and documents under the law, this will save you stress later.

Yes, "poor accounting" is one of the main reasons companies fail. You run your company blindly without bookkeeping or accounting.

Don't you still feel that your attention should be on bookkeeping? Fifteen reasons for bookkeeping are given below.

1. It Helps You Budget

Bookkeeping helps you keep your budget because it is good for your company. If revenue and expenses are properly organized, financial resources and expenses can be reviewed more easily.

A budget provides a corporate financial roadmap. You can plan future expenditures with a budget and anticipated resources covering those expenditures.

2. Tax Preparation

The company has to file a tax return every year in most cases. And every year, millions of company owners try to locate lost records from their desks. Sound familiar? Sound familiar? The process of filing taxes can be improved by simply having a bookkeeping function within your company.

Bookkeeping is also relevant when you file your tax return. A significant proportion of your profits as a business owner comes from your company. You need to know what your company earned first to know how much you got.

You will have financial records ready for tax time with a bookkeeping mechanism in place. Instead of searching for receipts or invoices, all your financial details are coordinated by a single central system.

3. It Helps With Proper Management

Good management is a capability that any owner of a company should have. You should always be able to find details about your business.

Some parties are interested in the financial records of your company-the IRS, employees, customers, investors, and lenders. It is essential for you to be able to provide the details requested by these parties. When you do not have documents obtained from the IRS, fines and fees may be levied. If the documents demanded by creditors or borrowers are not presented, this could mean a stop to cash flow. Being disorganized with your books can jeopardize or end your connections with these parties.

By definition, the management of financial information is bookkeeping. It is easier to find and support the correct parties by having the financial documents organized.

4. It Helps with Proper Analysis

The analysis is important as it helps with business analysis. This is a strategic tool used to assess organizational performance.

The bookkeeping tool is financial statements. Financial statements should be produced and used for review on a regular basis.

You can monitor your cash inflows and outflows when reviewing financial statements.

Bookkeeping provides you with knowledge about which businesses operate or not. This method of review helps you to concentrate on the strengths of your organization and strengthen its weaknesses.

5. Poor Decision-Making

Better decision-making comes with research. To make the best possible choices, you have to have access to all the information available. This knowledge is given by bookkeeping.

How can you expect strategic decisions to be made without financial information?

6. Planning Purposes

Bookkeeping shows the company's past financial results. Then, You must have a good understanding of the past in order to plan for the future. Bookkeeping offers you an idea of what works or doesn't work exactly.

Bookkeeping not only assists in strategic planning but also plays an important part in tax planning. This gives the CPA the information needed to categorize income and expenditures properly.

You and your CPA will arrange those expenditures more favorably through bookkeeping. For instance, if you regularly meet your customers, you may decide to have lunch at your meetings. This has favorable tax advantages for your business.

7. Simple Reporting to Investors

Investors want to know the company's financial results to quantify its investment value. That's what the financial statements say. Your company worth is all shown in the balance sheet, income statement, and cash flow statement.

As previously mentioned, the bookkeeping tool is financial statements. Investors may obtain up-to-date and usable information through bookkeeping. Investors may make smarter, smarter-informed choices that are the primary objective of bookkeeping.

Bookkeeping is not just for existing investors but also for future investors. If you have structured financial information, potential investors are more likely to invest in your business. Consider, would you invest in a business with no open and structured financial reports if you were an investor?

8. Financial Management

Bookkeeping is critical because it enables you to take over the finances of your company. Bookkeeping shows you clearly how you spend money. The outstanding invoices owed by you or your clients can be seen. You will benefit from the prompt payment of your bills and delivery of your products or services. The delicate balance between cash inflow and outflow keeps the business going.

9. Peace of Mind

Disorganized books as a business owner can weigh heavily on your mind. Your bookkeeping does not hold you up at night with all those aspects of running a company.

When your accounts are complete, you can rest easily assured the financial information from your organization is ready for review. Banks or IRS don't have to think about you anymore. Rather, you will find your mind more relaxed and focused on other components of your company.

10. Track Profit and Growth

Taking a proper bookkeeping record is important because it shows the productivity of your company. Let's, for instance, and the income statement is one of the bookkeeping financial statements. On the income statement, you will see whether or not the company is profitable. It is so possible to know how well (or not so well) you are doing without this knowledge.

Bookkeeping also contributes to growth monitoring. You can collect months and years of data over time. You can track patterns and better understand your business cycles and compare results over periods with these statistics.

11. Great Cash Flow

Effective accounting for cash flow increases the cash flow. The daily reporting of profits, expenses, liabilities, and receivables will help you to control the payment of invoices from your customer and seller. For a business, you want to ensure that customer invoices are paid promptly. Earlier, the better. The seller's invoices will always be charged promptly to discourage late fees.

How does bookkeeping allow cash flow to improve?

Since bookkeeping provides information about the unpaid invoices – the name of the client, number, issued date, and due date – that can be used to implement better cash flow policies.

Some examples are reducing the time that your customers can pay you. On the other hand, the payment of the seller's invoices can be delayed by waiting for one or two days before the due date. This increases the average amount of cash that you have at any time.

12. Greater Focus on Strategy

Strategic and tactical planning is the core of what you do as a business owner. You always look for ways to develop and grow your business. However, with proper bookkeeping as a tool, you are closer to your short and long-.

You should literally utilize the info that bookkeeping gives to concentrate on technique. Apparently, you can trace the results of your strategy with bookkeeping and adjust goals accordingly.

13. Offers a Snapshot of Your Business

accounts, in the form of financial statements, provide videos of financial details for your product. Financial statements such as the balance sheet, earnings statement, and cash flow statements all provide for a defined period of time financial details. However, these two statements take a snapshot of your company and show you the success of your company.

14. Easier IRS Audit

In the regrettable event, you are being audited by the IRS to ensure that the books are in order. Messy books prolong the auditing process, making the business more vulnerable to fines and penalties.

When the IRS thinks that the records are obsolete or disorganized, they have more justification for enforcing penalties.

In the case of an audit, it is better to make the task as straightforward as possible for what you ask in good time. If not, give them time to find more problems with your business.

15. Under Law

Last but not least, the law requires you to keep financial records for your company. The law mandates that you keep financial reports separate from your personal expenses, depending on your legal framework. If you fail to do so, your business will end.

What Next?

You now know how critical bookkeeping is. This will save you a headache, money, and time. If you need a bookkeeping process, consider hiring a bookkeeping professional to help.

Bookkeeping and accounting can be complex and confusing. Also, it may be difficult to identify a single transaction.

CHAPTER 2 :
FINANCIAL STATEMENTS

Here you'll see how financial statements are drawn up from your records and how their use will help you understand your company's financial position and recognize the relative strengths and weaknesses. Business owners who take the time to consider and analyze their transactions by financial statements over their lifespan will be well ahead of businessmen who only deal with goods or services.

What are the Financial Statements?

The past and future results are expressed in the financial statements. Such statements are both the basis of your tax information and how you assess your business. These are developed from your general documents and are divided into two key categories: Real Statements of Performance and Pro Forma statements. It is best to understand what financial statements are and who you can use for your business before you go further.

Real Performance Statements

These are the historical financial statements that represent your company's past success. You don't have a background if you start a new venture. However, if you have just one accounting cycle in business, you start generating these two financial statements, both of which are invaluable to you when you decide on your company. And these are:

1. Profit and Loss Statement
2. Balance Sheet

I'll also introduce you to a corporate financial report, which is a combination of the balance sheet, income & loss statements, and details on the legal framework. This is also used as a credit query.

Pro-Forma Statements

Pro forma means expected in accounting. These are the financial statements used to estimate the business 'potential profitability. Your forecasts are focused on objective analysis and rational assumptions that aim not to overestimate or underestimate your sales.

- Pro forma Cash Flow Statement (or Estimate).
- Quarterly Expenditure Analysis (means of calculating real budgetary results by Pro-forma measurement)
- Three-year Forecast (Pro Forma Earnings Statement)
- Breakeven Analysis

How to Get Started

Each of the following financial documents will be discussed: The data from these three statements would then be used on a regular basis to perform a quarterly budget review. A business plan would include some additional financial statements, which can act as valuable financial planning resources. Four principles for preparing financial statements in different cases are as follows:

1. If you are a new business, you'll look for a lender or an investor. You would have to write a business plan. All-Pro Formma statements included in this chapter must be made. You have no financial records and cannot provide recent performance reports.
2. Suppose you're a new company and don't look for a lender or investor. You still have to think about writing a business plan. All-Pro Forma statements are included. However, if you chose not to write one, your cash flow (budget) is extremely important.
3. Suppose you are an operating organization and are searching for a creditor or an investor. You would have to write a business plan. All the financial documents covered in this chapter and other elements will be included.
4. When you are an existing company and are not looking for a lender or an investor, all accounts are valuable. The statement on income and loss, balance sheet, and proform cash flow is a must.

What is a Balance Sheet?

A Balance Sheet is a financial statement representing the company's financial status on a fixed date. This typically occurs at the close of an accounting cycle. You may compare the Balance Sheet with a still photograph. This shows what your company holds and owes at a given time and whether your financial status is good or weak. By periodically reviewing this document, you will recognize and evaluate patterns in your business 'financial strength and then make timely changes. A Balance Sheet summary appears on page 65.

Format

The Balance Sheet must follow an agreed format and contain the following three sections so that everybody can read it readily. The three groups are related in that the assets of a corporation equal the total contributions of its shareholders and owners at all times.

Assets = Everything the company holds with monetary value

Liabilities = Business debts owed by any of its creditors

Net value (capital) = equity sum

The relationship between these three terms is clearly explained in a mathematical form.

Assets – Liabilities = Net worth

Reviewed as such, it is evident that if a company has more actives than its creditors owe, its net worth would be positive. Conversely, if the company owes investors more money than its assets, its net value would be negative.

Sources of Information

You (or your accountant) will produce a balance sheet on order using accounting software for your company. The numbers come from the general records when you do the accounting manually.

Description of Categories

- **Balance sheet**

Assets

Everything that your company owns or owes has a cash value.

- ***Current Assets***

Assets that can be turned into cash within one year of the balance sheet date.

- ***Cash:*** This is money; you've got money on hand. Require funds that have not yet been deposited.
- ***Petty-cash:*** Money deposited and not yet spent to Small Money.
- ***Accounts receivable:*** This is money you owe to sell goods and/or services.
- ***Inventory:*** This involves raw materials, work-in-process, and goods produced or bought for resale.
- ***Short-term investments:*** Stocks, shares, CDs (assets intended to be converted to cash within 1 year). List the expense or market value that is lower.

- ***Prepaid expenses:*** These are goods or services purchased or leased before use (e.g., deposit, insurance, inventory transactions prepayment, etc.).
- ***Long-term investments include:*** holding stocks, bonds, and special savings accounts for at least one year.
- ***Fixed assets:*** Capital owned and not planned for resale by a corporation

- Land. Original purchase price list. The land has not been depreciated.

- Buildings. List at cost, minus any previous depreciation.

- Tools, furniture, vehicles. Notice at depreciation cost reduction. To assess car worth, Kelley Blue Book can be used.

Liabilities: What the business owes; creditors 'claims on your assets

- ***Current liabilities.*** The liabilities accrued within one operating period.

- Accounts payable. – Accounts payable. Bonds due in one operating period.
- Payable notes. Short-term notes; list the principal balance due. List the present portion of long-term debts separately.
- Interest payable. Tax payable. Value in equity and liabilities earned.

- Taxes due. Estimated sums during the accounting period were incurred.
- Accumulated salaries. Present compensation and benefit liabilities.

- ***Long-term commitments***. Excellent balance less the current share due (i.e., mortgage, vehicle).

Net Worth (also known as "money" or "equity ownership").

The arguments of the owner/owner for the company's assets (document according to the business's legal structure).

- Contracting or alliance. The initial investment of each owner plus earnings after withdrawals.
- Company. The sum of the owners 'or shareholders' contributions plus the profits after dividends have been paid.

INCOME STATEMENT OR PROFIT AND LOSS STATEMENT

What Is a Profit and Loss Statement?

That statement shows your financial activities for a period of time, typically your fiscal year. Profit and loss statements can, as compared to the balance sheet, showing a picture of your company in a specific moment, be likened to a moving picture – showing what has occurred in your business over time. It's a great tool to assess your company. You will find flaws in your process and prepare ways of running your company more efficiently and thereby increase your income. For example, you could find that heavy ads you did in March did not increase your sales effectively. In subsequent years, you can plan to use your promotional funds more efficiently by using them at a time when consumer expenses are through. Likewise, you can review your profit & loss statement to see which months have the biggest volume of sales and schedule your inventory accordingly. Comparing your P&Ls over many years will give you a much clearer understanding of your market patterns. You should not underestimate the importance of this method during your tactics preparation.

How to Create Profit and Loss Statement

How to create a statement of profit and loss In contrast to the pro form accounts, which are estimates for future financial periods, the statement of profit and loss (Income Statement) is collected from actual business transactions. The P&L indicates where the money comes from and where it was spent for a certain time. And only at the end of the tax year, but at the end of the business month, should it be planned. It is one of the two major financial statements compiled from the media and the company reports. For the P&L Report, the balance between revenue and expenditures is used. The balance sheet statistics contained in the last three pages are presented with the remaining assets, liability, and capital details. Through multiple accounting, the profit balances, sales expenses, and expense accounts are passed to the P&L Report. When using software for accounting, you can produce a statement of profit and loss for an optional duration (current month, fiscal year, last fiscal year, date, etc.) anywhere you want. If your bookkeeper does so, a P&L Statement will be sent to your accountant at the end-of-each month as well as at the end of the tax year. When you set up a single entry with General Records, the P&L Report can be created by simply moving your income & expense report to the end of the month.

Type and Information Sources

The Declaration of P&L (or income) should also follow an agreed accounting framework for some categories. The following is the proper format and brief description of the things to be included in each group or estimates to be made in order to get to "the bottom line" or share of the income of the owner for the year.

Income:

1. ***Net sales/revenues (brut sales decreased revenues and allowances):*** What were your cash receipts during this period? If your accounting is accrual, how much did you invoice during the period?
2. ***Cost of goods sold:*** For estimates, see the form on page 69.
3. ***High profit. Small profit***. Subtract Net Sales Cost of Products.

Expenses:

1. ***Variable spending (sale):*** How much have you actually spent on things that are directly related to you? (Marketing, cost, freight, packing, travel, etc.)
2. ***Fixed (administrative) expenses:*** What sums were spent on the overhead office during the period? Net operating income: Good benefit minus fixed and variable costs (rental, insurance, payroll, office staff, telecommunications, internet services, etc.).

Other income: Interest during the time earned.

Additional expenses: Interest charged during the time.

Net profit) before taxes on income: Net profit from loans plus interest earned less interest paid out.

Income taxes: List of income taxes collected in the period (federal, self-employed, state, local).

After income tax, net profit (loss): Subscribe all income taxes charged in advance of income taxes.

BUSINESS FINANCIAL HISTORY

Your financial history is a financial document that is required before you prepare a business plan with a lender or investor. This is a rundown of your company's financial reports from the beginning to the present. The form is normally submitted by the lender.

- **If You're A New Business**

You can only have estimates for your company if you are a new business. The lender will need a Personal Financial History if you apply for a loan. In turn, this will be beneficial in that it will show him the way you worked out your personal business, an indicator of the probability of your success in your company.

- ***If You're An Established Company***

The application for a loan and your financial history are the same. The entity that provides the loan will provide you with an application if you suggest that you are keen on obtaining a business loan. Formats may differ slightly between lenders. When you receive your loan application, be sure to review it and consider how you will respond to each item. Answer all questions, and be sure that your information is accurate and easy to check.

Sources and Information Needed

Once you complete your Business Financial History (loan application), it should be immediately apparent why this is the last financial record to be done. All the information required was previously gathered in earlier parts of your plan. To help you with your financial history, the following lists usually contain information about your business and the source to which you refer:

- ***Capital, liabilities, net worth:*** All three are to be known as balance sheet requirements. You have already finished the company's balance sheet and now have to go back to it to put the dollar amounts forward.
- ***Contingent liabilities (i.e., the default of a co-signed note or settlement of a pending suit):*** These are debts that you may be owing in the future.
- ***Details of the inventory.*** Your inventory record extracts details. You will also provide a review of the existing inventory policies and appraisal methods in the organizational portion of your program.
- ***Profit & Loss statement:*** This is information about revenue and expenses. You must send the details from your annual profit and loss (last declaration completed) or from multiple compilations, if necessary, by the lender.
- ***Interest in real estate, stocks, and bonds.*** Respond to your plan's business section. You might also need to search your investment records for more comprehensive details.
- ***Title, association, or company details alone.*** There are typically three different financial history plans, one for each legal framework. You will have to fill in the one that is appropriate for your company. You have covered two areas in your plan's organizational section

that serve as the basis of this information: legal framework and management. Some of the information you will need can also be included in the supporting documents.

- ***Information on the audit.*** Refer to the Organizational Recordkeeping section. You might also be asked about other possible borrowers if you are obtaining loans, whether you are auditing your accounts and when they have been last audited.
- ***Risk insurance.*** Detailed information is required on the quantities of various coverage forms (i.e., products, appliances, liability, earthquakes, vehicles, etc.). The Organizational section includes information on financial history reporting.

PRO-FORMA CASH FLOW STATEMENT

What is a Cash Flow Statement?

One third or more of today's firms fail because of a lack of cash flow. This trap can be avoided by carefully preparing cash expenses. The cash flow statement (or budget) estimates for a certain time what your business needs in terms of dollars. This is a pro forma calculation (or projected) for internal planning and predicts how much money will flow into and out of business for a specified period of time, usually during the next tax year. Your income at the end of the year depends on the right cash inflow-outflow balance.

The cash flow statement shows when cash is to be earned and when bills and loans are to be paid for. This also allows the manager to decide where the cash is required. This statement only covers real cash transactions and does not deal with the depletion of goodwill or other non-cash expenditure products. Expenses are paid in cash, asset sales, sales and service income, investment interest, the money lent from a lender, and the capital inflow in return for equity within the business. When you need $100,000 to cover your expenses and $50,000 to help your family, you'll have at least the same amount of money to remain in operation. Anything less eventually leads to your creditors or yourself being unable to pay.

The fact that cash is available or not available when it is needed for expenses is at the heart of the matter. By careful preparation, you have to try to predict not just how much cash will flow in and out of your business but also when it will flow into and out of your company. An organization will be able to schedule gross receipts to meet its needs. Nonetheless, if these sales don't take place in time to pay the costs, a business will quickly be historic unless you intend to distribute your cash streams in advance before profits are realized.

Time period: The cash flow statement should be updated for the next fiscal year on a monthly basis. To be accurate, the actual performance must be evaluated and revised quarterly.

Planning Your Cash Flow Statement

It may be beneficial to compile individual estimates and budgets before preparing your budget.

- Estimates of sales (Product and Service)
- Inventory purchasing
- Variable (sell) budget spending (with marketing budget)
- Fixed expense budget

Preparation of Worksheets

Because the cash flow statement deals with cash flow and cash outflow, two worksheets will aid in the first phase of planning.

1. ***Cash to be paid Out worksheet:*** Cash from the company; defining cost categories and commitments and expected cash requirements in each category. Use your own budget details (inventory sales, variable costs, fixed charges, owner drawings, etc.). It is not always possible to estimate these expenses. When you are a new business, you will need to analyze the sector. If you are an established company, your past financial statements (such as P&L) can be combined with your industry trends.
2. ***Cash sources:*** cash flow into your business; used to predict how much cash from what sources will be available. You need to look at the cash on hand, expected sales, liquidated properties, potential lenders or creditors, and owner's equity.

To complete this worksheet, This worksheet will push you to look at any potential cash raise opportunities.

Description of Categories

Cash to Pay Out Worksheet

1. ***Start-up costs***

These are the costs you pay to get your business going. They are normally one-time costs and are paid for tax purposes.

1. ***Inventory sales***

Money to be spent on products for resale during the time. It requires the cash outlay on these sales when you buy manufactured goods. Require research and materials on units to be developed if you are the manufacturer.

1. ***Variable expenses***

These are all costs that are directly connected to the product or service (other than production or inventory purchase price).

1. ***Fixed expenses (administrative expenses)***

Include all overhead bureau expenses planned. When such payments have to be charged in advance, show the cumulative cash outlay, mainly though the protected duration lasts through the next year.

1. ***Fixed assets (long-term purchases)***

They are assets that are depreciated over a period of years (land, buildings, cars, equipment). Determine who you want to compensate to consider the cash that will be paid out for them in the present cycle.

1. ***Liabilities***

What are your fees to clear any obligations or loans? Do you have any payable accounts when you start the new year? You will need to determine how much cash is to be charged in the current year. When you've got a $20,000 auto loan and pay $500 a month for 12 months, you're going to have a $6,000 cash outlay over the next year.

1. ***Owner's equity***

This factor is frequently ignored in cash flow planning. When the business owner wants $2,000 a month to survive, you will expect to earn $24,000 cash from the company. When you fail to prepare, you will have a cash-flow shortage, and your business will collapse.

Note: Make sure you use the same time span for the worksheet.

Description of Categories

Sources of Cash Worksheet

1. ***Cash at hand***

This is the money you've got on your hand. Make sure you have small cash and not yet deposited money.

1. ***Sales***

It covers estimated profits from selling the product and/or service. Sales (profits) If payment in the duration covered by this worksheet is not planned, do not include this portion of your sales. Consider the planned timing of sales. When a large sum of cash is needed, make a report and take it into account when assessing the need for additional support when receipts are delayed. Have deposits for expected sales or facilities that you need. Once processing accounts receivable, you will have to estimate the number of invoices due to bad debt and deduct it from the overall accounts receivable.

1. ***Miscellaneous***

Do you have or are you going to have some loan money or deposits to accounts that will yield interest income for that period?

1. ***Long-term asset sales***

If you plan to sell your fixed assets such as property, houses, cars, equipment, etc., please ensure that only the cash you earn during this time is included.

1. ***Liabilities***

This is the amount you will borrow from lending institutions such as banks, financing firms, SBA, etc. You assume you should borrow fair. When you don't have collateral, a business plan, or a bad financial background, consider it difficult to find a borrower, if not impossible. This cash flow requires pre-planning.

1. ***Equity***

Capital sources come from owner contributions, contributed money, stock sales, or venture capital. Do you expect that personal funds will be available? Does your company have a growth opportunity that might attract a risk capitalist? Make sure you are practical. The stock (or equity) can not be sold to a non-existent buyer.

QUARTERLY BUDGET REVIEW

What is a Quarterly Analysis of Budget?

Your cash flow statement would be of no interest to you as a business owner unless there are certain ways to determine the company's actual output and calculate it accordingly. A quarterly budget review contrasts the estimated cash flow (or budget) with your company's actual output. It aims to show you how you operate in your project and help you maintain control of all phases of your venture. When your analysis shows you are over or below budget in any area, the cause for the deviation must be found, and adjustments made to get you back on track.

Example: When you've spent the first quarter of $1,000 on promotional funds and $1,600, you can first try to see if the increased advertisements have led to higher sales. If you had expected revenues of up to or above $600, your budget would continue to be in good shape. If not, you will include costs in the budget to make up the deficit. You may take a smaller draw or spend less on the trip. By introducing a new product or service, you can also be able to increase your income.

Format and Sources of Information

The following seven columns are needed for the quarterly budget review. Sources of information are listed for each entry column.

1. ***Budget-item.*** Project item. The list of items in the budget is taken from the Pro Forma Cash Flow Statement headings. All products should be specified in your budget.
2. ***Yearly budget***. Complete your Pro Forma Cash Flow Analysis for the current quarter.
3. ***The actual budget this quarter.*** Full the real quarter revenue and expenses. Those sums are included in your income statement, fixed asset file, owner draws, deposit record, or loan repayment reports.
4. ***This Quarter Variation.*** Total over or under budget expended or earned. Subtract the real revenue and expenditure from the sums budgeted to adjust.

5. ***Day to day budget.*** Year to date budget. Number forecast from year-early to quarterly inclusive (cash flow statement).
6. ***Present Year-to-Date.*** Specific sums expended or earned between the start of the year and the present fifth. Go to your General Records again.
7. ***Year-to-date variance.*** Subtract the amount that has been invested or earned from the current year and insert the difference.

THREE-YEAR INCOME PROJECTION

What is a Three-Year Income Projection?

The P&L Statement differs from the Cash Flow Statement as the 3-year forecast only contains expected earnings and deductible expenditures. This does not provide forecasts for non-income statements. The following examples indicate the difference:

- ***Example 1:*** The corporation plans to make loan repayments of $9,000 over the year, with an interest of $3,000. The entire sum ($9,000) will be reported on a statement of cash flow. Only interest ($3,000) is reported in a projected return. The principal is not deductible.
- ***Example 2:*** The organization wants to purchase a $15,000 cash car. The entire amount is reported in your statement of cash flow. The car is a depreciable asset and is reported only in the estimated income statement for the

year. You expect to earn $2,000 of owner draws every month. The draws are reported on your statement on the cash flow. These are not deductible and do not appear on the projected income statement.

Account for Decreases and Increases

Income and cost rises are just realistic and should be expressed in the forecasts. Accounting for raises and decreases Industrial patterns can also cause both income and expenditure decreases. An example may be the computer industry, in which relentless innovation, intense competition, and component standardization have triggered cost and selling price reductions of related services and products. The state of the economy will also contribute to your market outlook.

Information Sources

A three-year project can be built from your cash flow statement pro forma and your sales and marketing research. The estimates for the first year can be converted from the income and cost products. The second and third years are calculated from the combination of these quantities and expected patterns in your particular industry. Also, if you're an existing organization, you can use recent financial statements to help you find out what you need for your business 'future. Take into account expected variations in prices, operating performance, shifts in the market, etc.

BREAK-EVEN ANALYSIS

What is Break-even Analysis?

This is the point when the expenses of a product precisely equal revenue figures and where the business has neither benefited nor sustained a loss. By mathematical calculation or by constructing a graph, the breakpoint can be calculated. It can be measured in: total income dollars (exactly offset by total cost) – or total output units (costs exactly equal to the profits from their sales).

To perform a Breakeven Analysis for an operation, three projections are needed:

1. ***Fixed period prices.*** Most of these expenses are constant, even during slow periods. (Administrative expense + interest expenditure) Fixed costs for a breakeven study must be added to interest expenses.
2. Costs variable. (Cost of product + Expenses for sales) Typically differ with market volume. The larger the number of revenue, the higher the prices.
3. The average number of revenue.

Source of Information

All figures can be taken from the three-year forecast. Since breakeven is achieved when your total income equals your total expenses, you have to add enough years 'income and expenditure together in calculating the breakeven point so you can see that the total revenue is greater than the total expenditures. Recover and plug the figures into the following mathematical formula.

Mathematically

Sales at the breakeven point can be determined with this formula:

BE point (sales) = Fixed costs + [(Variable costs/East revenues)/refundable)]

Words used:

a. (Apparently, you will be able to see that each financial statement in your business plan is based on what you have previously done.) Sales = market volume at point b of breakeven. Fixed costs = operating expenses, amortization, interest c. Prices variable = prices of production and selling costs d. Estimated revenues = revenues (from goods / services sales)

Example:

a. S (BE point sales) = unknown

b. FC (cost fixed) = $25,000

c. VC (cost of variable) = $45,000

d. R (estimated income), = $90,000

Using the formula, the equation tends to be as follows:

S (at BE) = $25.000 + [($45.000/$90.000) [=

] = $25.000 + (1/2/to S) S–1/2 S = $25.000 + [[(25.000 $/ $90.000)] Free!

At least, we hope that you will be much more confident with producing a Pro Forma cash flow statement, income & loss statement, and a balance sheet of your own in your general records. These three documents are the backbone of your business. The remaining financial statements you have reviewed will also prove useful, particularly if you are drafting a business plan.

It takes time to know. Don't expect all this knowledge to be understood and absorbed at the moment. I'm sure you're overshadowed. All can be done as you set up and work on your documents. Recordkeeping isn't hard. It's all about repetitive jobs that will soon become commonplace.

Business Planning

I want to say another word on business planning before I finish this essay. Every now and then, I have listed the advantages of writing a business plan in the article. Most businessmen are shuddering about the structured planning process. It's a challenging challenge, but it can eventually affect performance and failure. Whether you are looking for a lender or an investor, a business plan is needed. Nevertheless, it is more important to follow the guide during the life of your company. After learning about record keeping and financial statements, you would have taken an important move forward in the planning process.

CHAPTER 3 : TAXES AND ACCOUNTING FOR SMALL BUSINESSES

Tax System and Accounting

To manage business bookkeeping, it is imperative for you to have a vivid understanding of your financial-tax accounting relationship. Accounting principles governed the implementation of the federal income tax. The aim was twofold:

- Accounting taxes. Your financial reports allow you to collect the required tax filing details at the end of your tax year.
- Reporting your income. Similarly, the tax forms to be submitted will give you valuable hints as to how your accounts are to be formed, not only in a functional format but in the way you will review your financial statements and evaluate the adjustments that need to be made for potential growth and benefit.

Relationship Between Business Analysis and Tax Forms

To better comprehend the relationship between the tax system and the analysis of your company, I will give you two examples of tax forms and how you can benefit from understanding those.

1. **Schedule C (Form 1040):** Benefit or Business loss (Sole Proprietorship) (Solo Owners 'mandatory tax reporting form).

- ***IRS information:*** gross receipts or sales, start- and end-inventory, labor, and supplies, purchased goods, returns and deductions, deductibles, tax payments, tax profits, and net profit or loss.
- ***Benefits of understanding:*** When you do not collect, the information you have provided above is exactly the same as the profit & loss statement list of revenue and expenses. If you have a return from the IRS, you simply pass details from profit and loss. Knowing this, you will look at Schedule C to see which information categories are required for expenses. This will help you determine which categories you are going to use in your revenue and expense report. It will also support you when your accountant returns you to the IRS for submission. You can now put your knowledge of the P&L Report to use and read and test it for accuracy – a job that taxpayers too often neglect. Because you are ultimately responsible for the accuracy of your return, knowing how to test it can avoid costly mistakes.

Note: Form 1065, United States of America. Return of Profit for Associations, Form 1120 or Form 1120-A, United States. Return of corporate income tax is used for such legal frameworks.

1. ***Schedule SE (Form 1040):*** Title Social Security Tax Computing.

- Required IRS details. Social Security commitment computation.
- Knowing costs. When you don't know the criteria to measure this tax and exactly what percentage of your net income is owed, you would be given a misleading image of your business 'net profit. Know, IRS is interested in your pre-tax net income. After income, you are concerned with net profit.

From the two examples, analyzing the tax forms needed will lead to discovering many types of records you may need and benefit from in your company.

Federal Axes That Can Be Liable

The next section of this chapter will provide you with tax calendars and outline the most common federal fees for which a sole proprietor, business, or organization may be liable. This section will also provide you with tax calendars. I do not give you full tax return details. I am trying to make you aware of the information required, familiarize you with some of the methods, and provide you with a structure for all your questions. I will send you a quick summary of will criteria, which include:

- Tax to report.
- Reporting forms used.
- IRS reports for information purposes.
- Each reporting form sample.

Federal Tax Calendars

I have issued tax calendars on the next four pages for your convenience. You will be used as a reference to tell you when tax and returns of information must be filed. -- of the four legal systems (single owner, partnership, business, and corporation) has a calendar. Take the calendar that matches your business and put it in your bookkeeping area to remind you to file on the correct dates.

The calendars are arranged in conjunction with different dates. If you do not have a fiscal year from 1 January to 31 December, the dates below the calendar are footnoted and can be translated into filing dates. These calendars are particularly useful in conjunction with your record-keeping schedule in the next chapter.

Using the Index

You will note that text and forms are indexed three ways at the back of the book if you are searching for details on a given tax or form: by form number, by subject, and by legal structure.

Income Tax (For Sole Proprietors).

Documents Schedule C (form 1040), Benefit or Company loss (sole-proprietorship). You are the sole owner if you are a self-employed individual and the sole owner of a business that is not incorporated. If you are a single owner, you report on Schedule

C, your company or occupation profits and expenditures, and report the net profit or losses of Schedule C on your Form 1040. You should file a separate Schedule C for each company if you run more than one company as a sole proprietor.

- ***Withdrawals:*** If you are an only shareholder, there is no tax impact if you take money from or to your company or move money from or to your firm. To track amounts for personal use and not business expenses, you should create a drawing account.
- ***Deductions from home offices:*** If you use part of your home solely and frequently to be the principal place of business or to treat patients, clients, or customers or communicate with them, you will subtract the expense of that portion of your home. When you seek a deduction from your home office, you need to submit Form 8829. (The sample form is included in Schedule C) See Publication 587, Your Home Business Use for more information.
- ***Estimated Tax:*** If you are a sole proprietor, you would have to make estimated tax payments if you have an estimated wage and self-employment wage of $1 000 or more for 2007. Form 1040-ES is used for the tax calculation. See "Solo Owners Estimated Tax."
- ***Self-employment tax:*** Generally needed if you are a single owner. See "Automatic Revenue," Schedule SE.
- ***Schedule C and Form 1040*:** Forms shall be submitted by 15 April. When you have a tax year, your refund is due

on the 15th day of the 4th month after your tax year has finished.

- ***Published by IRS:*** See publication 334, Small Business Tax Guide for tax laws discussion and examples to explain how these forms are to be filled out.

Home Office Deduction

Report Form 8829, Company Usage Expenses of Your Home (Schedule C). If you use your home for work, it is likely that you can deduct some of your business expenses. Yet you can not subtract more from your company usage than you earn in gross profits. The deduction is measured on Form 8829.

You must take other exams to claim a deduction for using part of your home in the company. That portion of your home you deducted from shall be used exclusively and frequently as (1) Principal place of business for the trade that you participate in, (2) as a venue to meet and interact with your customers in the normal course of your business or in relation to your business if you use a separate arrangement which is attached to, but not attached to, your home or house.

Note: The 1997 Taxpayer Relief Act liberalized the deduction from home offices for tax years starting after 31 December 1998. The new legislation expands the concept of the 'primary place of business' where: (1) the offices are used to perform administrative or management activities of the business or company of the taxpayer, and (2) there are no other fixed places for companies or entities where administrative or administrative activities are performed.

Measure Business Percentage

You have to split the costs of running your house between personal and business usage to determine deductions for the business use of your house. Many expenditures are split by region. Some of them are also separated over time. Divide the area used for the company by the total area of your home to find the business figure.

Deductible Expenditures

Certain costs, such as painting or maintenance in the same field of operation, are entirely deductible. Indirect use costs can be excluded, including property taxes, mortgage interest, catastrophe damages, electricity, telephones, insurance, protection systems, and depreciation. Unrelated charges are not deductible.

Form 8829: This form, entitled Your Home's Business Expenses, is submitted on 15 April with Schedule C (Form 1040).

INCOME TAX (PARTNERSHIPS)

File Form 1065, US Return of the Benefit of the Company. The partnership means the partnership between two or more people who work together, with each person contributing money, properties, jobs, or ability. Each of them expects to share in the company's profits and losses. Any company that does business or has income from sources in the U.S. must send Form 1065 for its tax year. This is mainly a return of knowledge. Profits from partnerships shall not be levied on partnerships. -- partner must take his or her share in the distribution of the partner's products into account and report on his or her own income tax return (whether or not distributed).

- ***Estimated tax:*** Tax on sales of partnerships shall not be withheld, and partners may be required to make estimated tax payments. For a self-employment tax, see Schedule SE (Form 1040).
- ***Self-employment tax:*** The distributive share of income of a partner is typically included in the calculation of net self-employment earnings. For the Self Employment Levy, see Schedule SE (form 1040).

Schedules K and K-1 (Form 1065): These forms aim to display delivery shares of reportable relationship products to partners. Form 1065 and its Schedules K or K-1 shall be paid separately and shall not be added to the tax return.

Part II of Schedule E (Form 1040) is used to disclose partnership items on the federal tax return. When you fail to comply correctly with your individual reports and relationship reports, the IRS will evaluate and take measures to obtain shortcomings and penalties.

Publication of the IRS: See Publication 541, Collaborations for information and examples of completed forms.

INCOME TAX

Tax Form 1120S, U.S. Tax Form 1120S. Revenue tax Return for a U.S. corporation. Some businesses can opt not to be taxed. When a corporation applies and wishes to become a U.S. corporation, its profits would usually be taxed on the shareholders. The establishment of a U.S. company is only allowed under certain conditions.

- It should be a domestic organization incorporated either in the United States or under federal or state law.
- It must have only one stock class.
- No more than 75 shareholders are needed.
- It must have only persons, properties, and certain trusts as shareholders. Partnerships and companies cannot be a U.S. company owner.
- Owners must be people or residents of the USA.
- The establishment of a U.S. business may be a beneficial legal arrangement, but when it is completed without proper preparation, it can lead to more taxes than less, as expected.

Form 1120S: This form is used to file a S company income tax return. Schedule K and K-1 are extremely important aspects of

Form 1120S. Schedule K outlines the shareholders 'earnings, deductions, credits, etc. Schedule K-1 indicates the separate share of each shareholder. The individual shareholders report on Form 1040 their income taxes. Form 1120S is due on the fifteenth day of the third month following the end of the tax year.

Publication of IRS: If you want information about U.S. companies, see Form 1120S Instructions.

INCOME TAX (CORPORATIONS).

Report Form 1120 or 1120-A, US. Return to Corporate Income Tax or U.S. Short Form Income Tax Return. The establishment of a company requires the transfer, in return for capital stock, of either assets, property, or both by prospective shareholders. Any company must file a tax return unless it is expressly exempt or dissolved, even if it does not have taxable income for the year, irrespective of the size of its gross profit. The company's earnings are normally paid to the client. If the earnings are split, the dividends are then paid to the shareholders.

Estimated Tax: Each organization is forced to make payment of the estimated tax if the overall tax is projected to be $500 or more for the year (with no credits). Corporations whose taxes surpass a certain amount (see rules) are obliged to make electronic deposits through EFTPS. All companies can choose to use EFTPS. If not, projected tax payments shall be deposited with a registered financial institution or depository of the Federal Reserve. For every deposit, Form 8109 must be included.

Capital investment of a corporation: Investments are "paying into debt" and are not the corporation's taxable income.

Form 1120 or 1120-A: For ordinary companies, the income tax filing is Form 1120. Forms 1120-A are for companies with gross sales, total profits, and total assets under $500,000. Also, there are specific requirements that must be fulfilled.

The returns of the business are due on 15 March. A company that uses a fiscal year not from 1 January to 31 December shall file the return on or before 15 days of the third month after the end of its financial year.

IRS report: See Report 542, Corporations to clarify how different tax laws (filing conditions and tax estimates, projected tax payments, distribution, and deferred profits, corporate tax debate, liquidations, and repayment of stock) are applied to companies. Publication 542 has completed examples as well.

ESTIMATED TAX

File Form 1040-ES (Estimated Individual Tax), (For Sole Director, Person Who is a Partner or a U.S. Company shareholder). If the individual, partner, or shareholder of a U.S. business is a sole owner, you will need to make estimated tax payments if the overall estimated income tax and self-employment tax is above a certain amount (in 2007, if it exceeds your $1,000 or more overall deductions and credits).

Underpayment of tax:

You will be expected to pay the penalty on the amount not paid if you do not pay appropriate income tax and self-employment tax for the current year by withholding or by making estimated tax payments. IRS is going to find out the penalty and give you a bill.

For the computation of your assessment, you use Form 1040-ES IRS Form 1040-ES. Four vouchers are released on 15 March, 15 June, 15 September, and 15 January. (Notice that between first and second payments, there are only two months, and between third and fourth payments, there are only four months.) Federal income tax and self-employment tax liabilities are included in the calculation.

You will use the projected tax worksheet to determine the total tax liability. Save your own records and check if your real income is well above or below your estimate. After the first filing, you will obtain the Form 1040-ES every year. For details, see Publication 505, Tax Withholding, and Estimated Tax. See also instructions on Form 1040-ES.

ESTIMATED TAX (CORPORATIONS)

File-Form 1120-W, Estimated Corporate Tax (Worksheet). Any business whose tax should be $500 or more shall make an estimated tax payment. A corporation's projected tax is less than its permissible tax deductions for its planned tax obligation (including alternative minimum taxes and environmental tax).

Deposits

If the estimated corporate tax is $500 or more, the estimated corporate tax payments shall be deposited with a registered financial institution or with a Federal Reserve Bank. A federal tax deposit coupon must be attached to each deposit and deposited as per the instructions in the coupon book. Deposit days are the 15th day of the 4th, 6th, 9th, and 12th months of the taxation year. Based on whether the condition for $500 is met first, a client may make either a deposit of four, three, two, or one payment. The estimated tax amounts will be reflected and updated each quarter to reflect changes.

Fine: A corporation that refuses to pay an annual tax in full by the due date is normally subject to a fine. The penalty is measured at an interest rate reported in the Internal Revenue Bulletin each quarter by the IRS.

Note: Corporations whose taxes are greater than a certain amount (typically $200,000) are required to make EFTPS (Electronic Federal Tax Payment System) electronic deposits of all depository taxes (such as job tax, excise tax, and income tax).

Form 1120-W (Worksheet)

This form is filled out as a method for estimating tax and deposits. The form will be held and not sent to the IRS. To help assess its approximate minimum alternative tax and environmental taxes, a company will obtain a copy of Form 4626-W.

Release of IRS:– See Release 542, Corporations. This paper concerns corporate taxes, settlements, and stock redemptions.

SELF-EMPLOYMENT TAX

(Partner, or S Company Shareholder) Report Schedule SE (Form 1040), Self-Employment Project.

The self-employment tax is a levy on social security and Medicare for individuals who are self-employed. The self-employed individual will benefit from social security just as they are for wage earners. Your self-employment tax contributions apply to social security coverage. This plan includes pension benefits and health insurance services (Medicare).

Note: You will be responsible for self-employment tax even though you are already fully Social Security covered and earn benefits.

Who is required to pay the tax?

Whether you have a company or service, except as an employee, you will have to pay self-employment income tax. A trade or service is usually a livelihood practice or a profit in good faith. The company doesn't necessarily have to make a profit, but it needs to have a reason for profit, and you will make regular efforts to support your company. Core elements are the regularity of operations and transactions and revenue generation.

Whether you are a sole owner, whether (1) an independent contractor, (3) a partner, or (4) otherwise in a company for yourself. You are a self-employed individual. You do not have to do a full-time daily business to be an autonomous job. In addition to the daily job, part-time jobs, even on the side, may also be self-employment.

Income Limits

You are expected to pay tax on self-employment if you have net self-employment earnings of $400 or more. The rate of self-employment tax for 2006 is 15.3% (for the Social Security net income, a total of 12.4% for 2006 up to a maximum of $94,200) (planned: $97,500 for 2007 and $10 1,400 for 2008) and 2,9% for Medicare on total net income. You would not be paid on the number on self-employment wages because you are also a payer and these earnings were subject to Social Security Tax.

There are three steps to determining the amount of self-employment tax that you owe: (1) calculate your net self-employment income, (2) decide how much is subject to tax, and (3) subtract that amount by a tax rate.

Note Two tax deductions related to self-employment tax on the income tax return. Both deductions are raising the net income tax burden.

1. By Schedule SE, 7.65 percent of the net income from self-employment is excluded directly from Schedule SE, which lowers the self-employment tax rate by that amount.
2. Type 1040. Type 1040. A deduction reduces your adjusted gross income in Form 1040 by allowing half of your tax liability for self-employment to be excluded as corporate costs. It is a change in income tax only. It does not affect your net self-employment income or your SE Tax Plan.

Joint Returns

Even if you file a joint income tax return, you may not file joint Schedule SE (form 1040). Your wife is not there because you are self-employed. You must use each file a separate Annex SE (Form 1040) if each of you has self-employment income.

Social security number

When you have to pay a self-employment fee, you will have a social security number. You may apply for one at the social security office nearest to you. Type SS-5, Social Security Card Application, can be obtained from any social security bureau.

Form SE, Self-Employment Tax (form 1040)

SE Form is used to measure self-employment taxes. When you are allowed to pay the statutory income tax, you will still have to claim any self-employment tax that you owe when you submit your 1040 ES vouchers. If you are not expected to pay estimated taxes, your annual tax return will return the full payment.

Publications of IRS: See Publication 334, Small Business Tax Guide. Read Publication 533, Self-Employment Tax, for more comprehensive information. An illustrated Schedule SE is included in the report.

Social Security Tax and Withholding Tax

File Form 941 (941E, 942 or 943), Federal Employees Quartal Tax Return. Forms W-2, W-3, and W-4 are also included. You would be allowed to deduct federal income tax from their wages if you have one or more employees. The employee's share and the related social security (FICA) and Medicare taxes must also be collected and paid. You are responsible for paying these taxes to the federal government, whether you receive them from your workers or not. See "Tax-Deferred Responsibility" on page 137.

Who is Employee?

By the common law, anyone providing services subject to the will and influence of the employer is an employee, both with regard to what needs to be done and how it needs to be conducted. The employer has the right to release workers, and the employer offers support and a place of employment, two aspects of an employer-employee relationship. No matter if the employee is referred to as an employee, partner, co-venturer, agent, or independent contractor. Whether the payments are assessed, how they are made, or what they are called does not matter. It doesn't matter whether the individual is full or part-time.

Note: See Publication 15-A, Employer's Supplemental Tax Guide, for detailed overview and descriptions of employer-employee relationships. If you want the IRS to decide if an employee is an employee, file the SS-8 form for your business position in the District Director.

The Federal Contributions Act (FICA) provides for a federal system for elderly people, survivors, disabled persons, and health benefits. Old age, survivors, and disability are covered by social security taxes. The portion of the hospital is funded by the Medicare tax. Each of these taxes is stated individually. You and the workers are paying social security taxes. For an employer, you must collect and pay part of the tax for the employee. You have to refrain from salaries. You will also be responsible for your own share of social security taxes (employer's share).

Employment Rate

Social security payroll rate for employers and workers is 6.2% each (a total of 12.4%), while the base pay for 2006 is $94,200 (wage bases are estimated to be $97,500 for 2007 and $101,400 for 2008). The Medicare tax rate is 1.45% each for employers and employees (total 2.9%). For the Medicare levy, there is no salary base cap. All earnings covered are taxable. Taxes on social security and retained income taxes are registered and charged jointly. Read Publication 334, Small Business Tax Guide, and Publication 15, Circular E, Employers 'Tax Guide for comprehensive information.

Withholding Income Tax

Typically, workers' salaries are withheld if their payroll salaries surpass the total sum of their withholding allowances reported for that time. For each payroll date, the sum to be withheld is shown separately. You will pay a gross wage withholding before any social security fee, pension, union duties, benefits, etc., deductions are made. The Employer's Tax Guide, Circular E, includes the correct tables and detailed instructions for using withholding methods.

Tax Forms

The forms used to record social security taxes, and deferred earnings tax are as follows.

File 941, Federal Employer Tax Return

Typically, Social Security (FICA) and Medicare benefits and income tax withheld are reported on File 941 - Forms 942, 943, and 945 are used for workers other than the regular form. Forms 943 (for farm workers) are an annual return due one month after the end of the calendar year. The remaining forms are quarterly returns due one month after the end of each quarter of the year. The due dates are 30 April, 31 July, and 31 October. An extra 10 days will be charged if taxes are paid in full and in due time.

You would usually have to make contributions to social security and medicare taxes and deferred income tax before the return is due. Form 8109, Federal Tax Coupon For taxes recorded on Form 942, no deposits are required. You will pay both your share of the Social Security Taxes and that of your employee at an approved financial institution or a Federal Reserve Bank. For information on deposits, see Publication 15, Circular E, Employer's Tax Guide. Federal Tax Deposit Coupons for forms 8109 are used for making deposits.

***Form W-*2**

Copies of Form W-2 are provided for each employee exempt from the income tax or social security tax. Form W-2 shows the total wages earned and other compensations. Social Security and Medicare Full earnings, payroll benefit, social security, and Medicare tax numbers, as well as all other information on this document. Detailed information on this form is given in the Form W-2 instructions. Provide workers with copies of Form W-2 as soon as possible after December 31, so that their income tax reports can be filed early. It must be forwarded to the employee on or before 31 January. W-2s do have to be sent to the Social Security Administration each year.

Forms W-3

Employers must annually send W-3 to the Social Security Administration forms W-2 and W-2P. The Social Security Administration must then process these applications and provide the Internal Revenue Service with the income tax data from the applications it needs. Form W-3 - attachments must be filed by February of the last day of the calendar year for which Form W-2 is prepared separately from Form 941.

Form W-4

An employee can typically claim retaining allowances to amount to the exact - exemptions someone has to claim on an income tax return. The new employee will provide you with a W-4 form, the Certificate of Withholding Allowance, on or before the first day of work. The certificates must contain the social security number of the employee. Copies of W-4, which are required due to a large number of deductions or claims for exemption from income tax withholding, shall be submitted in the form of quarterly returns for employment tax (Forms 941 and 941E). The withholds then measured on gross wages before social security benefits, tax allowances, insurance, etc. Responsibility for tax withheld. You are obligated by law to deduct and withhold income taxes from your workers 'salaries and wages. The federal government is responsible for paying the tax whether or not you receive it from your workers.

IRS Publication: Publication 15, Circular E, Employer's Tax Guide, for comprehensive information.

Unemployment Tax

State Form 940, State Unemployment Employer's Annual Tax Return. Using Form 8109 to make deposits as well. In accordance with the state schemes, the federal unemployment tax program allows for insurance for unemployment benefits for employees who have lost their jobs. The tax applies to the workers 'salaries. Many businesses pay the federal unemployment tax as well as the state. Generally, you are subject to FUTA wage tax for employees who are not farming workers or household employees if: (1) you paid $1,500 or more in any calendar quarter of your employees in that category or (2) there was at least one day, in each of your 20 separate calendar weeks, you had one employee in the following category; For lists of payments exempt from FUTA and the forms of jobs not subject to tax, see Circular E, Employer's Tax Guide.

Tax Calculation The federal unemployment rate is the first $7,000 annually paid in salaries to each employee. You, as the employer, are paying the fee. You will not raise or subtract it from the employees 'wages.

Tax Rate

The federal average unemployment tax rate is 6.2%. Nevertheless, the state unemployment rate you pay is compensated with up to 5.4 percent, provided you have met the state unemployment obligation by the due date. Therefore, the net tax rate will be only as small as 0.8% (6.2% minus 5.4%) if the country is subject to a credit reduction. Study rules relating to the responsibility of this tax (i.e., credit decreases, employer performance, related corporate concurrent employment). See publication-15, Circular-E, Employer's Tax Guide for information on the figure for Federal unemployment tax, including special "successor employer" laws.

For disclosing use is Form 940 Employer's annual FUTA tax return, Form 940. This form spans a calendar year and is usually due one month after the end of the year. However, before you file the return, you can have to make deposits of the fee. If you pay the tax in full on time, you need an extra 10 days to file – until 10 February.

Deposits If you ow, but haven't paid, more than $500 of Federal Unemployment Tax (FUTA) for the year at the end of each calendar quarter, a deposit must be made by the end of the next month.

Due dates are:

If your untax is over $500 on full deposit by 31st March. 30 April, June 30. 31 July 30 September 31 October December, 31

December. January 31 You do not need to deposit the tax at $500 or below at the end of the quarter, but you must apply it to the tax for the next quarter and deposit it under the law of $500. Use the federal Tax Deposit Book with Form 8109 federal tax deposit coupons to deposit taxes in an approved financial institution or Federal Reserve Bank (See publication 15, Circular E, Employer's Tax Guide)

Form 8109 For deposits to an approved financial institution or a Federal Reserve Bank, federal tax coupons are used. The names of licensed institutions can be obtained from a Federal Reserve Bank. The Federal Tax Deposit (FTD) coupon must be included in each deposit. Clearly mark each coupon for the appropriate form of tax and tax duration. The FUTA revenue will be paid separately and income tax contributions withheld. After you apply for an employer identity member (EIN), a federal tax cup containing Form 8109 cuts and directions will be automatically sent to you.

Publications of IRS: Form 940-FUTA Tax Return (Instructions), Publication 15, Circular E, Tax Guide of the Employer and Federal Tax Deposit Coupon (Instructions) Form 8109.

Services Rendered

File Form 1099-MISC, Notice to Special Revenue Recipients, along with Form 1096, U.S. Annual Report and Transmission Payment. Returns of knowledge. The payments you make for your company or non-wage activities must be reported to the IRS. Payments include fees, bonuses, incentives, awards, or other types of compensation for the services given by a non-employee to your organization. This often involves fair market value in exchanging property or services (trading) between individuals during a company or business. Exempt payments cover inventory fees, real estate agent rental payments, phone service payments, insurance, payroll payments, employee travel expenses, and company payments.

Form 1099-MISC

Declaration to the recipient for Miscellaneous Income is a form used to record payments to non-employees (or who were a nominee/middleman, or who have been exempted from federal income tax or external tax) in the context of your trade or company.

On or before the last day of February, when and how to register Form 1099-MISC? Transmit these forms with US Form 1096, Annual Review, and Transmission to the IRS Support Center. Returns of knowledge. A copy of the 1099-MISC shall be sent to the receiver by 31 January. For cash payments, file Form 1099-B, Broker and Barter Exchange Proceeds.

Publications of IRS: Publication 15-A, Supplementary Tax Guide for the Employer. See the guidelines for forms 1099 and 1096 for more detail on 1099s in the current year.

TAXPAYER ID NUMBER (EIN)

Form SS-4, Employer Identification Number query.

Social Security Number (SSN)

When you are a single owner, you usually use your Social Security Number as your taxpayer identification number. You will write this number on each of your income tax forms, such as Form 1040 and schedules.

Employer-Identification-Number

Any partnership, S company, company, and some single owner must have an employer identification number (EIN) for use as a taxpayer identification number. EINs must be open only to proprietors who are paying one or more workers or have to file pension or excise tax returns. They will use their social security numbers otherwise.

New EIN

You can need to request a new EIN if either the business form or ownership changes.

- ***Organizational transition.*** A new EIN is needed if the sole owner has a partnership; the sole owner is a partner, operating as a partnership; a partner takes over one partner and acts as the sole owner. A change of partnership or a sole owner becomes a company.
- ***Change of possession.*** You must acquire or inherit an existing company that operates as a single owner's company; you are representing an estate that operates a

company after the death of the owner, or you end an old relationship and establish a new one.

Request for an EIN or Social Security Number

Using Form SS-4, Work Identification Number Request for an EIN. This form is available from the IRS and the offices of social security. The form can be accessed online as well. To do so, go to www.irs.gov and enter Form SS-4 in the search box to the page where you can access the form in pdf format.

For a Social Security number card, Form SS-5 is used. Both forms are accessible from the Administration Offices of Social Security. In case you are under 18 years of age 18, you must have proof of age, identification, and U.S. citizenship along with this form. In case you are 18 years old or older, you must appear in person at the Social Security office with this documentation. If you are an immigrant, your birth certificate and your immigrant identification card or US immigration form must appear in person.

FREE TAX PUBLICABLE OF THE IRS

A list of IRS publications that may be helpful for you during your business cycle is listed below. Make sure you have a tax details log. Send these publications and refresh your file at least once a year with new publications. The government of the United States has spent a lot of time and money writing income tax returns for you.

Through telephone or mail: You can call IRS at 1-800-TAX-FORM (1-800-829-3676) at no additional cost from 8-5 p.m. and from 9 a.m. to 3 p.m. on saturdays. You will find an order form for the publications on page 151 if you want to order publications or forms by email.

By device and modem: If you sign up for an online service, ask if information about IRS is accessible and, if so, how to access it. IRS provides the possibility to download electronic paper files in three separate file formats, including existing tax forms, guidelines, and publications on taxpayers' information (TIPs). FedWorld's Internal Revenue Information Services (IRIS), also known as the U.S. Government Data Technology Exchange, is a commonly distributed online newsletter program. FedWorld offers direct networking and Internet communication, and "gateway" links to more than 140 government newsletter boards.

IRIS can be reached by any of the following methods:

- Modem (Dial-up) System 703-321-8020 (not toll-free) Internal Revenue Information Systems
- ***Telnet:*** http:/iris.irs.ustreas.gov
- Link to http:/ftp.irs.ustreas.gov
- File Transfer Protocol (FTP)
- World Wide Web — www.irs.gov

Small Business Tax Guide (S or S-EZ) Alone should start with a reading of Publication 334, Small Business Tax Manual. This is an overview of all small business sectors and provides you with detailed knowledge.

Listing of small business publications

If you are a small company owner, the following IRS publications are useful for you as reference material and provide you with very detailed information on various tax-related topics.

Summarily, It is vital that you keep track of changes to tax laws that affect your company.

IRS Workshops

The IRS periodically conducts tax sessions for small business owners interested in finding out more about new laws and criteria. You may contact the nearest IRS office to submit a list of workshops to be issued.

Know What is happening

Making plans for your company is an evolving process that needs several changes to be carried out. You should be assured that all of these changes would result directly from new tax legislation. Most small companies will have to rethink their employment policies because of new regulations on workplace insurance, workers 'compensation, contract services, etc., that has been implemented or proposed. Business owners have to consider what is happening and take constructive actions in order to influence policy that is important to their activities and can eventually be successful or failing.

You took the first step. If you had already dedicated yourself to organizing and knowing your documents, you should not read this book. However, you're one of the fortunate ones – entrepreneurs realizing that every decision has an impact on the final analysis.

However, when the following four (4) conditions are met, the following payment is usually stated in the form of non-employee compensation: (1) you paid a non-employee; (2) you paid for services provided within your business; (3) you paid a non-business pay; and (4) you paid the payer for a total of $600 or more in the year.

ACCOUNTING FOR VAT

Nearly anyone who operates a business will be paying Value Added Tax (VAT). This chapter discusses what it is, how it affects you, what documents you have to keep, and why.

Value Added Tax

The Value Added Tax (VAT) is a 17.5% capital spending levy. The old purchase tax regime was adopted on 1 April 1973; it was partially harmonized with the taxes paid by countries of the EEC (now the EU). The tax is regulated by HM Customs & Excise (not domestic income).

VAT has an effect on certain facets of your trade, and you have to decide whether to register your company for VAT purposes and how to manage your accounting documents for additional details. The chapter, therefore, offers a description of VAT in order to give you an idea of what is involved.

How VAT Works?

Under VAT, every corporation is simply a tax collector. The fee for the selling of goods or services by a business licensed for VAT is payable. (Specific purchases are excluded from VAT or charge a zero fee.) The VAT rate is currently 17.5% of the price of the product on any other purchases. Such purchases are referred to as taxable products, and the value-added tax you have to apply on your sales is called the income tax. Instead, if a registered company purchases products (or services) from another registered manufacturer, that company shall pay the VAT that is paid to the other company. This sales tax is referred to as the production tax.

A company licensed for VAT has to pay the sales tax less the input tax to the Customs & Excise. When the income tax is higher than the sales tax, the difference between customs and excise will be recovered.

Example:

Assume a store buys an \$80 wholesale radio; an extra £ 14 input tax must be charged to the wholesaler. If the shop sells the radio to a buyer for £ 100, an extra \$17.50 is paid, and the customer is paid \$117.50 for the shop. The shop will then pay the difference between tariffs and imports \$3.50. As you can see, the radio value in the shop has risen by \$20. That is the added value bit. The net effect of the tax payment (for the difference between the exit tax and the input tax is to tax the added value of the business-\$ 20 x 17,5 percent = \$2,50. The premise is that the name of the tax is issued.

How Vat Affects Your Business

Do I need to declare my business for VAT?

Note: VAT-free or foreign supplies are not part of a taxable turnover but are inclusive of supplies paid at a zero rate. If the amount of your taxable turnover over the past 12 months exceeds \$61 thousand at the end of any month, OR (b) you have reasonable grounds for assuming that the value of the taxable products you produce in the next 30 days exceeds \$61 thousand, then you have to report your company for the purposes of VAT.

You have to inform the Customs & Excise VAT Office that within 30 days following the end of the month, your company has reached these limits. The registration will then take effect from the first day of the second month after that (for example, if your taxable turnover is over the mark in the last 12 months before January, the registration date will be 1 March). You can easily inform them by using the national VAT aid line. The number is 0845 010 9000.

When you take over an existing company, the amount of taxable turnover under the previous owner will be taken into account. The filing date will be the day the business has been sold.

When your revenue falls below the mandatory registration cap, you can also apply for VAT when you think it would be a benefit. For example, you can sell to other companies that are registered for VAT themselves. You will get the input tax back on your sales by registering your own business; while you have to charge your customers with VAT, you will, of course, be able to get it back. When you buy and sell only zero-rated goods, you can still register to assert the input taxes paid on your expenses (e.g., vehicle costs, telephone costs, professional fees, and so on.

What if I have more than one business?

Note that the 'individual' is registered for VAT and not the company. When you run more than one company, even if they are different, and the taxable turnover of all companies reaches the defined limits together, you must register for VAT. All companies are protected by one registration and cannot be registered separately.

How do I get VAT registration?

You will fill in the VAT form 1. If your business is a partnership, you must also complete a VAT 2 form, which shows each partner's names and addresses. These and other forms and information can be found at your nearest VAT office (see the telephone directory for VAT or Customs & Excise).

What documents do I have to hold once I've registered?

It will partially depend on the type of company you operate. Yet summaries will require you to include the following details:

- The value of the sales income tax
- The value of income tax on purchases
- The total sales excluding VAT
- The amount of all transactions except VAT.

How often do I need to advise my purchases on Customs & Excise?

The specifics of transactions are not personally reported to Customs & Excise: they would be swamped with a sea of paper! Alternatively, you collect the data for a period of three months, and then notify them of the total amount of the VAT return for the duration (form VAT 100). To spread the workflow throughout the year, licensed traders are split into three categories by their business form. These are referred to as stagger groups, and each group returns on a different date.

Group 1 Group 2 Group 33 April 30 April 30 June 30 July 31 August 30 September 30 November 31 December 31 January 28 February

These quarterly cycles are referred to as periods of VAT accounts. The Customs & Excise will tell you in which category you are going to be.

The Customs & Excise uniquely enables a registered individual to make returns monthly instead of quarterly. It will benefit if the company results in regular VAT refunds. You can also seek an adjustment of the accounting periods to suit the business year. Contact your local VAT office for more information.

How long will I fill in the VAT return?

The VAT return must be submitted and forwarded to the VAT office within a month of the end of the VAT portion. If you are late, you are in default and receive a note of surcharge. This will inform you that you might have to pay a penalty surcharge if you are late again. Whenever you default, the penalty rate increases to up to 15 percent of your VAT. This hazard persists until a full year has passed without default. If your revenue is less than £ 150,000, however, the fines will not always be imposed; rather, before such action, advice and assistance will be given.

How do I finish the VAT return?

A series of boxes are included in a standard VAT shape (VAT100):

- Box 1 is for sales VAT production tax. You must also include a value-added tax on goods purchased from the business for private consumption, the motor fuel price (see page 60), and asset sales (e.g., machinery, office equipment, etc.).
- Box 2 the VAT due on imports from other EU countries is reported.
- Box 3 shall be the number of boxes 1 and 2, respectively.
- Box 4 the VAT input tax on your sales is shown.
- Box 5 varies from boxes 3 and 4. It reflects either the VAT on account of the customs and excise duties (if box 3 exceeds box 4) or the amount that you say (if box 4 exceeds box 3).

The VAT offices use the figures in boxes 6 to 9 to generate statistics and test the figures shown in the other boxes of the type.

- Gross revenues minus VAT are shown in Box 6.
- Box 7 indicates the gross company costs minus VAT and any other expenditures such as salaries.
- Boxes 8 and 9 are used for the reporting of trade with other Member States of the EU.

Detailed guidance notes are given at the back of the return. More specifics are given later in the chapter regarding the completion of the return form.

What are retailing arrangements?

You may have read of supermarket schemes. These are special schemes for use with retail supplies only.

The retail schemes offer a way to achieve the amount of taxable retail sales and to assess the proportion of sales to the various VAT levels. Many VAT licensed businesses take this details from their customers 'sales invoices. However, this is not feasible for retailers due to the vast amount of transactions made directly to their public.

The amount of retail sales must be registered in all retail systems. In most schemes, you calculate your sales value-added tax by adding the VAT element to the correct proportion of your revenue.

There are five common schemes:

- The point of sales scheme. At the time of sale, transactions are measured using an electronic till among the different VAT prices. It is the most detailed, which involves costly equipment and personnel who know-how.
- The distribution systems.
- Scheme 1: sales are split into the purchasing ratio. If 40% of your orders are zero, then 40% of your profits are considered zero.
- Scheme 2: figure out the estimated retail prices for all the items you sell, and then determine by adding the correct

ratio the proportion of sales at each VAT rate. This scheme can be difficult to run but more concise than Scheme 1.

- The systems for simple measurement

- Scheme 1: Under this scheme, the average retail price of 'minority products' is calculated, and the standard valued prices chargeable to VAT can be defined with this amount specified. Thus, if 85% of your sales are normal, and 15% are negative, you have to measure the estimated sales revenue from the negative (minority) sales. The number of sales paid at the regular VAT rate can be calculated by deducting this figure from total sales.
- Scheme 2: operates the same way: operates in the same way as Scheme 1 so a wider variety of retailers can use it.

Specific modifications are made to the catering and retail chemists' schemes. You should contact your nearest VAT office for more information about these schemes and ask for flyer 727.

What's the odd fraction?

Fraction 17.5/(100 + 17.5) is used to describe the VAT value of a gross product (including VAT).

Using a VAT rate of 17.5%, the cost of the goods plus the VAT shall be 100% of the retail value (i.e., the cost of the products) plus 17.5% of the VAT net value. Consequently, the total gross revenue will be 117.5% of the net costs of the goods minus VAT.

If you are trying to find the VAT stuff, 17.5/117.5 would be the total sum of the products, including VAT. (Note: this is not equal to 17.5 percent of the gross amount.) Basic arithmetic is used to make it easier to deal with (but not much) the 17.5/117.5 fraction at 7/47ths. We will presume that you have a pocket calculator! This fraction is referred to as the VAT fraction.

Do I need to provide all my customers with VAT invoices?

In general, yes, you must give your customers comprehensive invoices. The information you need to give is this:

- An identification number (this is common in order to list the invoices sequentially to each one having a unique number)
- The date of delivery (tax point)
- The name and address of the person to whom you deliver the goods (or services)
- A description of the products or services that are supplied by the VAT provider.

Unless the invoice includes information about products or services, which may be common in certain situations, and which may be nil (or exempt), then the invoice must differentiate between the items paid at each cost. Nevertheless, you just have to send invoices to those customers who submit a tax invoice if you are a retailer. In addition, adjusted Tax Invoices can be issued as follows: If a gross value (including VAT) does not exceed £ 100, the retailer's name, address, and VAT number only have to be specified the following: date of sale (tax point) of the products, the overall value includes the VAT rate paid.

Where goods surpass £ 100, a changed invoice form may be provided showing the VAT-inclusive value of the standardized goods if the customer so agrees. The description of the value of the goods (distinguishing between zero-graded, regular valued, and excluded supplies), value-added tax, and total payment must be given. It must be like a tax invoice in all other respects.

Recording Vat Transactions

The VAT program overview has already been addressed, so we will review the records you need to keep in case you are VAT registered.

The standard way to compensate for VAT is by the time of supply or by revenue. This is explained below, but for VAT traders whose annual turnover is less than £ 660,000, there is the option of a cash accounting basis. We're going to come later to this.

The usual basis: scheme of tax points

The time you have to pay for VAT is usually determined by the date of delivery or the tax point as it is called. In the VAT era in which the goods or services are rendered, VAT must be accounted for. It can, of course, not be the same as the time when a credit period is paid for.

Sales and Output tax

There are two facets of reporting VAT on transactions, namely:

- The details you must include in your sales invoice.
- The information you must include in your account books.

If you do not use any of the retail systems, you need to keep a separate record of your sales in order to calculate VAT income tax. Finally, before the company outstrips the program, an exercise book will document the transactions: no costly specialized book is needed. Please enter the info periodically from your copy invoices. Reference points:

- Use the reference number. You can also record it on the copy invoice and allow you to recognize each invoice.
- Log in net, VAT, and gross amounts. Such amounts should be shown clearly on your invoice. The net amount shall be the product's value before applying VAT; the total value shall be the value after VAT.

Remove the columns at the end of the VAT cycle to get your VAT refund. The sum of the 'Net' column will be entered as the 'Price of Outputs' in box 6 on the VAT Return, subject to any changes. Inbox 1 of the VAT return form, the complete VAT column should be entered as 'VAT Due.'

Import Tax on Transactions

Again, when you use one of the retail schemes, the VAT record book is somewhat close to the one used for sales. However, it is worth adding a rundown of the cost (purchases, telephones, engine expenses, etc.) because that will help you plan your accounts at the end of the year.

On the VAT return, the total column of 'Net' is used to complete box 7 (Input value). Inbox 4 (VAT Deductible), you insert the sum of the VAT column on the form.

Note: Certain items should not be included in boxes 6 or 7 and should therefore not be included in the VAT books.

- Salaries and Wages
- National Insurance Contributions and PAYE

What's Next?

Now that you know the basic documents, financial statements, and tax returns, it is time to combine your information and to use it to formulate record-keeping schedules and tax returns for your company. Building and holding the documents up to date are two separate things.

To help you start the next chapter, you will be given written guides as you get used to performing all the unfamiliar tasks needed to keep your records current.

CHAPTER 4 :
RECORD KEEPING IN SMALL BUSINESSES

Now, you will understand the interaction of every recording level. To this point, the following have been introduced:

Record-keeping basics:

- Tracking functions and forms
- At the beginning of record-keeping and who will do so

Important records for small companies:

- What records are needed
- What are the purposes of records
- Drafting of financial statements

Taxes and Record-keeping

- Publications available as tax aids
- Forms to be used
- Federal taxes for which you can liable

Development of financial Statements

- Introduction sources
- What they are

- How they are developed

Organizing Your Record-Keeping

You cannot put all the documents into a basket haphazardly and treat them sporadically. You will coordinate your record-keeping into a method that allows you to continue orderly during the fiscal year. The program will provide you with tax information to be collected and checked at the same time as developing a picture of your business that will allow you to identify patterns and make adjustments to expand and make your company more profitable.

Creating your framework

For a specific purpose, the material in this book has been delivered in a particular order. Just as a homebuilder must first lay the foundation, build the foundations, bring the walls up and finish, you must also build the foundation and learn the fundamentals of recordkeeping. The system can be applied to your documents. These are the fundamental material in which no walls can exist. Likewise, general documents form the basis of the creation of financial statements (source of information). Finally, the builder completes the house and turns certain rooms for each family member and other rooms into common areas where the whole family is going to meet. The tax accounting system operates within its restricted areas but is practiced in areas common to all businesses. The house is complete – and the record-keeping is complete. There is now a plan to maintain your home, or it will soon be a shamble. To keep the business in a maintained condition, it also has to be maintained. In order to ensure optimal maintenance, you need to create a record-keeping and tax reporting schedule.

If you believe that you never reported and you have no idea how it must be done, I'll give you a simple format to follow as you learn this mission.

Doing Tasks in Sequence

There is a certain order to log, and you must obey that order if your records are to be accurate. Because the two goals of recordkeeping are tax retrieval and internal planning review, the timetable must provide for achieving those objectives.

However, on the rest of the pages, we have included a general record keeping and tax reporting plan that will only be fulfilled if you follow it. To ensure success, you have two things to bear in mind:

1. Don't miss any of the activities.
2. Make sure you do it on time.

Post your schedule on the wall of your office and talk about what needs to be done every day. Such functions will become automated in the near future. All the information presented in this book is taken in mind, and you start to see the picture as a whole. If you follow the plan at the end of the year, you will have all the financial details at your disposal. This can be done – and it can be done!

Schedule format

The General Schedule is divided into frequency assignments. Two main divisions exist:

1. ***General Record-keeping***

- Daily. The things you do when you keep your books daily. Timing can vary depending on your business needs.
- Weekly. The timing might vary according to your business need.
- Monthly. At the end of the month, close your books.
- Quarterly. Study of the last quarter and budget review.
- Year's end. Close your books for the year and set new year records.

1. ***Collection of taxes***

- Monthly. Payroll reports and deductions, recording of sales tax (sales tax can be monthly, quarterly, or annual).
- Quarterly. Sending the tax reports needed.
- Each year. Filing tax returns and records.

Each organization has its own needs. You can need to adjust the pace of such activities. However, in the beginning, follow the progress in the timetable we have made, and this should adequately cover most of your needs.

Notice for the Various Legal Structures

Because some record-keeping activities vary for various legal structures (i.e., sole ownership, partnerships, S company, and corporation), the applicability will be noted. If the function is not followed by notation, it refers to all legal systems.

Respond back if you need help. Bear in mind that all things in the schedule have been addressed in one of the previous parts when you use the general record keeping schedule. You just need to refer to the document, declaration, or tax return details to refresh your memory and complete your mission. Please ensure that reference materials listed in these sections are kept close by if you need more detailed information.

Use these timetables!

The following schedules should be your reference before you learn the recording process. There may be other jobs to do, but you should make a good start.

Recordkeeping Schedule

Daily:

1. Go through the mail and prepare for action.

2. Unpack and eliminate inventory.
3. Inventory History Inventory Data.
4. Pay any invoices needed for discount periods to be met.
5. Report daily invoices sent to receivable accounts.

Please note: It would be a good idea to keep copies of invoices in an envelope or folder behind the respective receivables record.

*The accounting software: invoices created from software are automatically posted to the correct accounts.

Weekly:

1. Prepare and carry the bank deposit to the bank for income earned.
2. Join checkbook deposit and Revenue & Expense Journal.
3. Enter sales in Inventory Record.
4. Enter the week's Profit & Expense Report checking transactions.
5. Record small cash transactions and receipts in small cash records.
6. Pay due to invoices. Know the dates of the discount.
7. Register in your Fixed Asset Record all depreciable purchases.

* Accounting software: enter deposits, signed checks, and small weekly cash.

Monthly:

1. Clear checkbook (bank statement reconcile).
2. Write in your checkbook and Profit & Expense Report any tax charges and bank charges.
3. All columns of the Revenue & Expenses Journal.
4. Total monthly income and expenses in the 12-month P&L report. Prepare a separate benefit & loss for one month if you like.
5. Prepare a balance sheet if you want to look at assets and liabilities. Only those who are not sole owners or filers of Schedule C are needed at year-end (see Year-end).
6. Check Accounts Payable and submit accounts open statements.

* Accounting- software accounting. Perform reconciliation with the bank. Generate a P&L Report and a current Balance Sheet per month and year.

Quarterly:

1. Do a quarterly review of the budget. Compare actual revenue and expenditure with forecasts.
2. Test your statement of cash flow (budget) accordingly.

End of the Year Tax

1. Pay the invoices, sales taxes, and other charges you intend to use for the current tax year as deductions.

2. Prepare annual return on profit and loss. (Add total revenue and expenditures from the twelve-monthly reports.)
3. Prepare the company's balance sheet for all but sole-proprietors or filers of Schedule.
4. A balance sheet is required. Prepare next year's Pro Forma Cash Flow Statement (budget). Use your current year's income & loss information to help you make decisions.
5. Build your new records for the next year. However, it is somewhat a good idea to buy new reviews and files before the offer expires. Start recordkeeping for the first week.

* Accounting-software: Generate an annual profit and loss statement and a year-end balance sheet.

New Year Accounting does not need to be re-established. It will start last year.

Tax Reporting Plan

The following tax reporting plan is not intended for final use. Requirements can vary. You may also be liable for reports and returns not specified below. It is intended only as a general guide to help you keep track until you know the exact specifications for your business.

Note: This schedule applies to the reporting days and tax returns. Apparently, there are tax reporting calendars for all legal frameworks in the tax chapter. Upload your schedule and refer to the schedule for the forms and dates requested. Also, refer to descriptions of individual forms mentioned in the index by subject and form number.

Monthly:

1. ***Check your payroll tax liability:*** If you surpass $2,500 for a quarter, you will have to pay a refund for the taxes of the preceding month on the 15th day of each month. (If you are dealing with an accountant or payroll company, you can provide them with reports on payments and amounts of maintenance as early as possible during the month so that you can receive back details about your deposits.)
2. ***Sales tax reports:*** You can need to file your sales amount monthly, quarterly, or annually. In some cases, you may have to be signed or paid in advance. Complete and send the State Board of Equalization's sales tax report (or in certain countries, sales tax may be administered by the Department of Revenue) with a check for the amount received (or payable) for the selling, in the preceding year, of taxable products or services. It extends to all businesses with a seller's license. This book does not address the issue of sales tax. The report forms are supplied by the collecting agency and will normally be due about 30-days after the end of the reporting period. (See our company

launch book, Steps to Small Business Start-Up, Kaplan Publishing)

Quarterly:

1. Taxes calculated (Form 1040ES). Register with the Internal Revenue Service projected taxes. If appropriate, you must also file with your state.

- Sole owner, partner, or S member of companies reports on the fifteenth day of the fourth, sixth, and ninth month tax year and on the fifteenth day of the first month after tax year-end. The due dates will be April 15, June 15, September 15, and January 15 for most corporations. If the due date is on a Sunday, the next Monday is the due date.
- Companies shall register the 15th day of their fiscal year on the 4th, 6th, 9th, and 12th months. Then, it will be April 15, June 15, September 15, and December 15 for most companies; the same rules apply for weekends.

Note: Note that between the 1st and 2nd quarter of the filing, just two months pass. Between the third and fourth quarter-finals, there will be four months.

1. ***FICA and Receivables (form 941):*** Quarterly Federal Tax Returns File Employer's Social Security Reporting

(FICA) Payroll and Receivable. Check early to see if deposits are needed.

2. ***FUTA deposits (Form 8109):*** Allow tax deposits of Federal Unemple (FUTA). Failure to make deposits on 30 April, 31 July, 31 October, and 31 January, even if outstanding tax liabilities exceed $500.
3. ***Sales tax reports:*** If you report on a quarterly basis, then reports for the previous quarter will be due by 30 April, 31 July, 31 October, and 31 January. Unless you are only expected to file annually, it is normally due for the previous calendar year on 31 January.

Yearly:

1. FICA and withholding returns of details. Provide social security information (FICA) and income tax withholding information. (To notify the client of any relevant regulatory requirements)

- W-2 for workers on 31 January
- W-2 and W-3 to the Department for Social Security on the last day of February.

1. 1099 returns of information. Submit non-employee payment information and transactions with others.

- Forms 1099 by January 31st due to the receiver.

- Type 1099 and 1096 IRS transmissions on the last day of February.

1. Tax returns for FUTA. File Federal Tax Returns (FUTA) with the IRS. The date is 31 January.
2. Income tax return (Form 1040). Income tax returns. File IRS (and your state, if applicable) income tax returns.

- On the 15th day of the fourth month following the end of the tax year, the person who is a partner or the corporate shareholder file (generally April 15, Schedule C, Form 1040).
- Then, returns that are due on the 15th day of the 4th month following the end of the year of the relationship (generally on 15 April, Type 1065).
- Companies (1120S) and companies (1120S) register on the 15th day of the third month following the end of the tax year (generally 15 March).

1. Tax forms for self-employment (form SE). Tax forms for self-employment are filed under Form 1040 (see above).

- Only owners or individuals who are partners.
- Self-employment forms only occur if the taxable income of your corporation reaches $400.

CHAPTER 5 : PREPARING FOR YOUR TAX RETURN

This book will not be full without providing you with details on getting ready to file your returns on income tax. As stated earlier, one of the two key purposes of record-keeping is the collection and verification of income tax.

When all your research at the end of the year is over, it's time to start focusing on income taxes. I'm not saying you do it yourself. Nonetheless, I highly recommend that you hire a CPA, licensed agent, or other tax professional to plan and help you optimize your tax benefits. Not all of us are well enough educated that all tax laws and adjustments will be in good order. Yet you should do a lot of the preliminary work. This will help you in two ways: (1) You will save your accounts, and (2) by focusing on your taxes, you will learn a lot about your business.

There will be considerable variance in what you can do yourself, not just because of the nature of your particular company but because of the individual's ability to maintain records. That is why we do not seek to provide advice on the preparation of preliminary taxes. However, we can give you some sound advice at this point. You also spent the year recording and filing financial statements. They are the documents that hold all the details you need to pay for income tax. In fact, you could actually fill out your own tax return if the IRS rules were not so easily updated and complicated.

However, since you need a skilled preparer to ensure your return is right and optimize your rewards, it is your responsibility to collect and distribute the information required to do the work.

Many tax preparers are complaining that the job is difficult because clients do not prepare their content. They carry bags full of receipts and documents. How do you need the accountant to prepare?

What to Give Your Accountant

Your accountant would have the requisite details from sources you would already have if you have maintained your general and financial statements.

For All Businesses:

There are two things your accountant wants from you irrespective of your company type:

1. ***Annual profit and loss statement:*** This lists your accountant with all the income and expenditures the company has earned for the fiscal year. If you are in a commodity business, you would have to measure the cost of the products sold for your return. You will make a start

and end inventory each year. You will need the following items before you complete your P&L statement:

- Starting Inventory: Inventory as of 1 January of the current year. It must suit the figure described last year as "finishing inventory."
- Closing Inventory: Inventory as of 31 December of this year. This is achieved by a physical warehouse. It will be the first inventory for the coming year.
- Amount of stock purchased: List the expense of all stocks that your company bought during the fiscal year.

Note: When you are making your own P&L document, you can calculate the "Cost of goods sold." Furthermore, it would help to test your comprehension and consistency if your accountant has a list of the three things listed above. When you use the software, the P&L statement can not include the inventory beginning and end. You will also need to provide the accountant with these figures for "Price of products sold."

1. ***Copy your Asset Log Fixed.*** This document lists all the company's depreciable assets acquired during the current year, date of acquisition, purchase price, etc. The accountant wants to ask if you've listed any of these factors in your P&L Report as expenditures (instead of factors for goods). You will also agree whether these things would be depreciated or spent under section 179.

Home-Based Company

List of home-based expenses. Because such items are usually charged on personal checks, details on income, insurance, and interest payments must be received (rentals, if not a home-owner). Maintenance and utilities are also required. Please ask your accountant to clarify the recapture if you sell afterward before you agree to depreciate your home as a deduction from a home office. You will have to estimate your office space and calculate the percentage of your home used exclusively for your service. In case you are claiming a home office deduction, your accountant needs this information to fill out the correct form to accompany your income tax declaration.

Partnerships, S Corporations, and Full Company

Owner Equity Draws Record

The three legislative structures listed shall have a return balance sheet detailing each owner's equity. In order to calculate the equity, the accountant needs to have each owner adding and withdrawing the sum. Use last year's balance sheets as a reference, deposits are added, and deductions are subtracted to the owner's new accounts. These amounts are generated automatically by software users.

It is best to tell the accountant as soon as possible after the new year. It offers additional flexibility for any questions you may have during the planning of your returns. You can also ignore sales taxes and continue the new business year.

The Last Chore

The IRS, in general, mandates that all records concerning income tax be retained for a three-year period from the date of filing of the return. Past returns are subject to audit during that time (and longer, in some cases such as fraud). However, for longer periods, some documents are kept, often decided by administrative decision. This is a smart idea to preserve all of them for your company's existence. Note that the other aim of records is to examine patterns and to enforce changes. It is only useful if it is still in your hands.

I found it very successful in collecting all the details for a year. In your file, mark it with the date of the year, and put it away.

- Income tax returns
- All payments receipts
- ATM reports
- Tax & Expense journal
- Petty-cash record
- Inventory of real assets, inventory report, etc.
- Every other information that is pertinent to verification of return.

CHAPTER 6 : THE PARTNERSHIP AND THE CORPORATION

The Partnership

The partnership is an 'association of two or more co-owners of a benefit company,' according to the Uniform Partnership Act. In general, the partnership arrangement is the same for the sole proprietorship, but with respect to the equity of ownership. The partnership uses each partner's capital account and drawing account. The relationship is defined by the following:

1. ***Co-partnership papers.*** The good business practice calls for a formal partnership agreement, with arrangements for partnership formation, allocation of each partner's money, sharing of benefit and losses, acceptance and removal of partners, removal of funds, and the dissolution of the company.
2. ***Unlimited responsibility.*** Both partners are unlimitedly responsible for and responsible for the obligations of the relationship. The company's obligations may be covered not only by the partnership's assets but also by the partners 'personal assets.
3. ***Property Co-ownership.*** All land invested in the company by the partners and purchased by the

partnership funds shall be equally owned by both partners. Therefore, in accordance with its capital balance, each partner has an interest in the partnership instead of a claim on particular assets.

4. ***Involvement in profits and losses.*** In accordance with the collaboration agreement, gains and expenses are divided between the partners. When there is no compromise, income and losses will be divided equally.
5. ***Restricted life.*** A relationship can be broken by insolvency, a partner's death, a mutual agreement, or court order.

Partnership Structure

The partner's capital account is compensated for their initial investment when a partnership is formed, and the corresponding asset account is debited. Investments of non-cash assets should be reported at an agreed amount.

Net Profit and Loss Partnership Division

The income and expenses of the can be broken down in some way that the partners can decide on. A partner may typically be required to share the amount of capital and/or resources it contributes. However, in the absence of a reason agreement, the legislation requires that both spouses share equally regardless of the devoted time gaps or the contributed money. The key methods of profit and loss allocation are listed below:

- ***Capital or Fixed Basis***

In general, fixed or capital base profit and losses are divided equally in a fixed ratio or ratio based on capital contributions from partners.

- ***Interest Basis***

Under this system, the interest on each partner's capital investment shall be paid, and the remaining net profit shall be split in a fixed percentage or on another basis. Therefore, the position of a partner depends on its capital investment.

- ***Salary Basis***

The parties may agree to accept contributions in the form of services, while the resulting net profit can be divided evenly or in a fixed ratio.

- ***Salary-Plus-Interest Basis***

The profit division is collectively determined by services provided to the company and capital allocation. Growing partner is paid a salary and interest on capital at the same time. If there is still some variance, it is divided into an agreed ratio.

New Partner Admission

The Uniform Partnership Act states that a partner can, without the consent of the rest of its partners, dispose of part or all of his interest in a business. The person buying the interest will be entitled to a share in income and expenditures by the selling party. This buyer is not, however, a full partner because, when he or she is admitted to the company, it has no vote and has no right to engage in partnership activities.

- ***Admission by Interest Purchase***

If a recipient buys an interest of another partner, the purchaser charges the purchase price to the old partner directly. The only adjustment needed in the accounts of the partnership is a transfer of capital from the account of the old partner to the account of the new partner. The company's assets and liabilities are not affected.

- ***By Contribution of Assets***

The new partner will add assets to the partnership, thereby growing the business 'assets as well as its resources. For some situations, when a new partner is accepted, assets can be revalued first, or goodwill must be remembered to align existing values with the capital accounts. This method is referred to as asset revaluation. The book values of all relationship properties must be modified before agreeing with current rates. In compliance with the income division arrangement of the former spouses, the net sum of the revaluation should be allocated to the capital accounts. If a number of assets tend to be needing re-evaluation, whether to higher or lower numbers, changes can then be made to an Asset Revaluation temporary account that is then shut down to the partners 'capital accounts.

Where a company has the capacity to receive more than the normal rate for its investment (due to favorable position, proven credibility, management skills, or better products or services), it is possible to imply goodwill and charge an incoming partner for it. If so, it shall be debited while the accounts of the old partners shall be credited in the ratios specified by the articles of partnership. On the other hand, if the incoming partner generates goodwill, it debits the goodwill account and credits the new partner's capital account.

Partnership Liquidation

Partnership winding-up When a company's partner wants to stop the business activities, certain accounting measures are necessary:

1. The accounts are changed and shut down.
2. Each asset is transformed into cash.
3. All investors are fully compensated.
4. Any cash left is allocated among partners in accordance with the capital balances of their accounts (not their profit-and-loss ratios).

The Corporation

It is basically an external body that is formed by legislation and has an ongoing life independent of its evolving membership.

Members are the shareholders; they own the company, but they are different from it. As an independent legal entity, the company has all of the rights and obligations of a person, such as contracting, suing, and litigation on its own behalf and the purchase, selling, or possession of the land.

Corporate Terminology

As owners of the company, shareholders have the right:

1. Voting (one vote for each stock share held)
2. Profit-sharing
3. Pass control of property
4. In the case of liquidation, share in the distribution of properties.

The Executive Board shall be elected by the holders under the Articles of Incorporation. The functions of the Board include the appointment of corporate officers, the development of company policies, and the distribution of profits.

A stock share reflects a unit of the company's interest. The par-value is an arbitrary number set out in the charter of the corporation and written on the front of each stock certificate. This entirely has nothing to do with the market value, that is, the actual purchasing or selling price. There are several stock categories:

1. Allowed shares are equity shares authorized to be issued by a company under its articles of incorporation.

2. Unsubsidized shares are registered securities not yet available for sale.
3. Subscribed shares share to be bought at a particular price on a certain date by a buyer. The shares are not distributed until full payment is received.
4. The treasury stock comprises shares issued and subsequently purchased by the firm.
5. The remaining stock is the equity approved, issued, and retained by the shareholders. (The corporate form is not exceptional because it is owned and not retained by the corporate shareholders.)

Benefits of the Corporate Form

In the United States, in contrast with sole ownership or partnership, corporate form has a variety of significant advantages:

1. The liability of the stockholders is limited. Every shareholder shall be responsible for the sum he invests in the company. If the company fails, the borrowers can not usually look beyond the company's assets to resolve their claims.
2. Effective ownership transfer. The ownership of a company is expressed by stock certificates; these enable shareholders, without interfering with the management of the corporation, to buy or sell their interests within a

company. Millions of shares exchange hands every day through coordinated transactions.

3. Existence persisted. A partner's death or incapacity can dissolve a partnership, but the life of a company is independent of its shareholders.
4. Legal body. The corporation will prosecute and appeal, contract, buy and sell on its own behalf. This is contrary to the sole ownership, which in all legal matters, has to be used by statute by individual names.
5. Ease of capital raising. Advantages 1 and 2 make the company an appealing stockholder investment. Compare that to the partnership, where the number of members, the sum of its own assets, and the possibility of limitless liability are restricted to raising money.

Drawbacks of the Corporate Form

While the business model has the benefits mentioned above, it also has some drawbacks, such as:

1. ***Taxation.*** The corporation has to pay federal income tax in the same way as an individual, resulting in dual taxation of corporate income. Double taxation is created firstly by the taxation of net profits and secondly by the share of profits allocated by individual income to the owner.
2. ***Organizational cost.*** When establishing this type of ownership, the company must obtain state recognition

and legal protection. State-to-state requirements vary; however, every State requires (a) a minimum stockholders 'number, (b) a minimum capital sum, and (c) incorporation fee and tax payment. The legal costs in question will amount to thousands of dollars in large corporations and must be applied to the expense of government services and taxes.

3. ***Legal limitations.*** The company's charter is the foundation of the transactions of the company and allows it to participate only in certain activities specified or implied in the document. Unless the corporation wants to operate in a foreign State, it must either register or pay a tax to the State.

The Equity Accounting for the Corporation

This is distinguished from the sole shareholder or partnership accounting by treating the owner (stockholder) stock, which is split into paid-in capital and retained earnings of a company. The explanation for this difference is that most states bar businesses from paying dividends other than profits. Money paid in is further divided, and so we have three main accounts of income:

1. ***Capital stock.*** This account shows the par value of the corporation's issued stock.
2. ***Additional Cash Pay-in.*** Amounts paid in excess of the stock market value.

3. ***Retained profits.*** The accumulated income from the successful operation of the company.

Common Stock

If a company issued only one stock class, it is classified as common stock, with all shares having equal rights. The ownership of a common stock share is entitled to:

1. Vote in the election of managers and in other significant business decisions.
2. Participate in the profits of the business.
3. Buy a proportionate proportion of potential stock issues.
4. Share in liquidation properties.

Preferred Shares

The company may also sell preferred shares to cater to a wider audience. This class of stocks does not usually have voting rights (although a special clause in the charter often granted these rights), but as its name implies, in several ways, this stock favors common stock.

1. ***Prior argument against profits.*** The Management Board has the power to declare and allocate dividends to the shareholders. In such allocations, preferred stock claims are honored before common stock claims. Nevertheless, the dividends paid to preferred stocks typically amount to the amount paid to common stocks.

From the accounting point of view, the biggest advantage of preferred stock is its value in collecting dividends.

2. ***Prior to asset claims.*** When the remaining funds after all shareholders have paid out are not enough to repay the full amount of the capital investment of preferred and common stockholders, following the liquidation of a company, payment must be made to preferred stockholders first. Any balance will then be made available to common stockholders.

The following options may also be offered to preferred stocks:

1. ***Call privilege.*** The issuing party has the right to redeem the stock for a fixed price at a later date. This call price will be above the original issue price, for example, 105% of the par value.
2. ***Privileged conversion.*** At their choice, stockholders will turn preferred stock into common stock. This could be achieved if the common stock of the company is more attractive than the preferred stock due to large profits.

Stock Problem

- ***Par Issue***

When a corporation is organized, the charter specifies how many common and favored acts are approved. More stocks are often allowed than should be sold immediately. This will allow the company to grow in the future without the State being required to issue more shares. The security entry is the usual form when the stock is sold for cash and immediately issued: cash is debited, the security is credited. In exchange for stocks, a company can accept property other than cash. If this occurs, the assets should be reported at fair market value, as usually defined by the company's board of directors.

- The problem at a Premium or Discount

There are several factors influencing stock market rates, such as:

1. Potential power to receive.
2. General terms of company and other opportunities.
3. Financial standing and record earnings.
4. Dividend record. Dividend record.

If the investors are willing to pay the excess or premium, the stock will be sold above par. The premium is not a benefit for the company, but rather part of the stockholders 'investment. If the buyer does not pay by value, the Company can issue an inventory below par at a price.

Book Value

The book value per share is calculated by dividing the equity of the shareholders by the amount of outstanding shares. Therefore, it is the amount to be allocated to each share of the share if the corporation is dissolved. Specific book values for the common and preferred share shall be specified by splitting the equity sum of the shareholders into two parts and by dividing the corresponding number of shares per part. Both rates and discounts and retained earnings or deficits are only applicable to ordinary stocks.

Earnings Per Share

The net profit after taxes is limited to earnings per share (EPS), except for any preferred dividend. It is equivalent to the income available to ordinary stockholders. Divide by the number of shareholdings outstanding to EPS:

- EPS: (number of common stock shares outstanding) /

Bond Characteristics

A Company can obtain funds by selling stocks or by bending by long-term borrowing. Bond issuance is a form of long-term debt under which the corporation agrees to pay interest on a daily basis and repay the principal at a defined future date.

Bond denominations are typical $1,000 different. A bond issue usually takes 10 to 20 years, although some issues can take longer lives. The day a bond is to be reimbursed is known as the maturity date. In a serial bond issue, the maturity dates are distributed over the period of the issue in a sequence. This alleviates the company from the effect of the full payment at one time.

Funding by Bond Vs. Funding by Stock

The key distinctions between stocks and bonds can be summed up as follows:

Stocks:

1. ***Representation:*** Corporate ownership
2. ***Holders Induction:*** Dividends
3. ***Accounting care:*** Dividends are income distribution; securities are equity
4. ***Repayment:*** Securities are always sold on the market

Bonds:

1. ***Representation:*** Corporation's debt
2. ***Holders 'Induction:*** Interest
3. ***Accounting:*** Interest is an expense; bonds are long-term liabilities
4. ***Repayment:*** A default date

CONCLUSION

Businesses have specific reporting responsibilities to state, regional and local governments. We have other conditions for public reporting to creditors and investors. Finally, internal reporting mechanisms for planning and monitoring are used. The federal reporting standards include labor surveys, payroll surveys, and social security taxes for salaried workers. Employers pay their workers unemployment taxes. The federal government has provided that banks and federal depositors receive taxes received by and from employees. In compliance with the IRS rule, the employer shall deduct federal income tax and social security taxes and pay them to a federal depository. Annually, the IRS requires employers to record salaries and taxes charged and denied to their employees. There are different reporting provisions for federal tax obligations depending on the type of the company organization. Sole ownerships, corporations, and associations pay a corporate company income tax. Nevertheless, S companies and partnerships file returns of details. As a different legal body, companies are charged.

Certain reporting standards derive from the existence of the business. For example, firearms dealers are strictly licensed and controlled by the US Treasury. Other firms are limited to selling prices, fees, and services. Providers, transport companies, banks, and other industries of this kind are strictly regulated. Some are closely supervised because of the risks associated with working conditions. Coal mining, chemical industrial industries, and airlines are only a few of these operations. Many companies and activities are also regulated and taxed by state governments. States typically tax the real estate of corporations and structures attached to the property through their ad valorem taxing authority. Machinery, machinery, facilities, and inventories of a corporation may be charged through personal property taxation. Intangible personal property taxes govern intangible ownership items such as inventories, bonds, and notes. Sales and sales made in other countries are, in some cases, taxed. For other nations, other goods, such as food, medication, and telecommunications services, are excluded.

Taxes, regulatory standards, and zoning limits on the activities of certain companies can be levied by local governments. Some counties or municipal governments may have concession provisions for the provision of services, such as exclusive access to cable TV services. Creditors have or are searching for other details to ensure the possibility of payment. Balance sheets, financial statements, and cash flow statements should be drawn up and circulated. Investors are also worried about these studies.

Eventually, businesses have internal preparation and monitoring reporting standards. These requirements vary with the scale, type of business, and management style used.

www.ingramcontent.com/pod-product-compliance
Lightning Source LLC
LaVergne TN
LVHW022051200926
848481LV00003B/867
* 9 7 9 8 2 0 1 1 4 3 2 2 0 *